D1323006

Paws Under the Table

While the pubs featured in this book were dog-friendly at the time of visiting, changes of ownership or other circumstances may mean that dogs are no longer welcome.

To ensure your dog is welcome and that the pub is open on the day you plan to visit, you are advised to phone and check before setting out. There is contact information at the end of the book.

The author and the publisher have done their best to ensure that the information in this book is accurate at the time of printing, but cannot be held responsible for errors or inaccuracies.

Readers should keep to public rights of way at all times, and the description of land, a building, a path or another feature in this book is not evidence of a right of way.

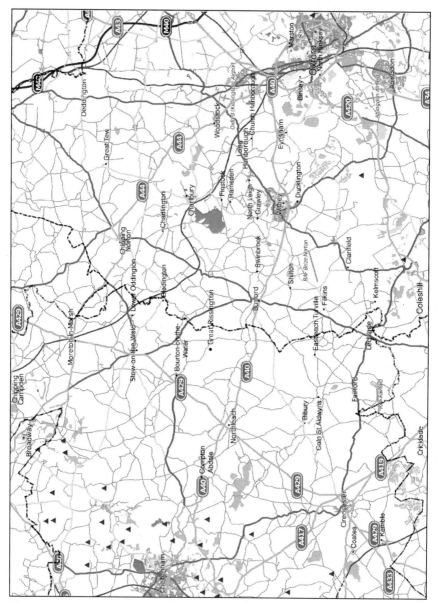

Map © openstreetmap.org and contributors

Paws
Under the Table

40 Dog-Friendly Pubs and Walks from Oxford to the Cotswolds

Helen Peacocke

Illustrated by Sue Mynall

Photographs by the author

To dear Anna with all best Wishes Helen Peacocke

THE WYCHWOOD PRESS

Dedicated to my father Alfred Harper Richards who shared his youth
with a dog named Silvio

The great pleasure of a dog is that you may make a fool of yourself with
him and not only will he not scold you, he will make a fool of himself too.
Samuel Butler (1835–1902)

Our books may be ordered from bookshops or (post free) from
The Wychwood Press, Alder House, Market Street, Charlbury, OX7 3PH
01608 811969

e-mail: orders@wychwoodpress.co.uk

All our books may be seen at www.wychwoodpress.co.uk

First published in 2009 by
The Wychwood Press
an imprint of Jon Carpenter Publishing
Alder House, Market Street, Charlbury, Oxfordshire OX7 3PH

ISBN 978 1 902279 35 0

Printed in England by CPI Antony Rowe Ltd., Chippenham

Contents

Who is Pythius-Peacocke?

If Helen hadn't opened *The Oxford Times* one Friday morning and noticed an advertisement for border collie puppies, perhaps Pythius-Peacocke would have remained at Mushroom Cottage and become a working sheepdog, at Slade Farm, Kirtlington, because he likes sheep.

But she did and when they met it was love at first sight.

The moment the kindly farmer who had bred him opened the kennel door and asked which puppy Helen would like, four excited little creatures leapt towards her, eyes sparkling, tails wagging.

'That one,' she said, pointing to a tri-coloured puppy standing a little back from the others, looking rather bewildered at this sudden intrusion. Then his eyes suddenly locked with Helen's. From that moment on Pythius-Peacocke's life as a companion-dog had began.

He's called Pythius because Helen's previous dog was named after the Apollo Theatre in Oxford, having been found stuffed into a dustbin outside the stage door when he was just five weeks old. According to Greek mythology Apollo the God bore the epithet Pythius after slaying the serpent who dwelt in the caves of Mount Parnassus. By giving Pythius this name Helen felt she was keeping the dynasty alive. And why Peacocke? That's simple – Helen wanted to give him the dignity of a surname.

Pythius-Peacocke's writing career got under way the day he noticed an article in *The Times* denouncing Border collies. The journalist dared to suggest that anyone buying a Border collie puppy at the farm gate had rocks in their head.

Pythius-Peacocke responded immediately. Sent a letter and his photo to *The Times* declaring that that the journalist had got it all wrong, as Border collies are very clever dogs if their intelligence is respected and they are treated with kindness.

It was published the following week. Within five days Pythius-Peacocke was receiving letters from Border collies all over the country congratulating him on standing up for this noble breed – and so his writing career began. Even now, eight years on, he regularly corresponds with Lovejoy, a kindly Border collie from Scotland, and Douglas from Cleveland.

Helen's duties as food writer for *The Oxford Times* include reviewing Oxfordshire pubs, so once Pythius-Peacocke had settled down in his new home, she invited him to join her on these visits. He liked some and disliked others, but gave them all tail-wag ratings. This book lists 40 pubs that he enjoyed most.

Pythius says

I can't say that living with Helen is easy – but it's certainly fun.

The food is good; I get regular walks and am probably the most knowledge-able dog in the country when it comes to pubs. I have come to know a bit about real ale too – not its taste, but its aroma. We visit at least one different pub a week. Sometimes it's just Helen and me, and sometimes it's Helen, me and Auntie Liz and very occasionally we go with someone else.

Whilst I am never allowed beer in the water bowl that's often provided by the publican, I do get to sniff that glorious mixture of malt and hops that goes into Helen's glass.

There are rules I have to obey however. When we enter a pub I have to go straight under the table and stay there until the meal is over, because most pubs that allow me in have strict rules about dog behaviour. Some publi-cans have their own dogs, and I learnt to respect them quite early on in our travels, as they often take their role as Top Dog very seriously.

There are rules governing the walk too. I have to follow the Country Code, stay close to Helen at all times and come straight back when called, even when I have discovered a glorious smell that warrants further investigation.

These are the rules I have to follow:

- Once the walk has begun I have to stay under close control at all times, most particularly when walking a bridleway or byway in case we meet a horse. Helen says she's responsible and I might frighten the horses and cause an accident.
- I must be on a lead or under close control when we approach farm animals too. Apparently a farmer has a right to destroy any dog that injures or worries the animals.
- I must not jump over walls, or rush through holes in hedges and must wait patiently while Helen closes farm gates securely once we have passed through them.
- I am not allowed to wander into areas where ground-nesting birds are nesting – particularly between March 1 and July 31, as vulnerable species such as skylarks can be easily disturbed if I don't stick to the footpath.
- I must always wait for her to put me on the lead when we approach a road and must never dart out into the road without her.

Rules that Helen has to follow when I am accompanying her:

- She must always keep a bottle of cold water in the car and provide me with a drink of water whenever I need one.
- She must never, EVER, shut me in the car on a warm day and leave me there while she goes shopping.
- She must strap me into my doggie-safety harness whenever we go for a drive.

The Swan Hotel, Bibury

Bibury is one of those picturesque Cotswold places that everyone should visit at least once in their lifetime if only to lean over the low stone wall of its main street and simply take in the unspoiled beauty of the River Coln and the sight of the celebrated cottages in Arlington Row. These weavers' cottages, built in local stone and now owned by the National Trust, are probably the most photographed buildings in the Cotswolds.

On visiting the area, car-maker Henry Ford was so impressed with the cottages he tried to buy the whole row to ship back to his history

Pythius says

Who would have thought that a classy hotel such as this would allow dogs to put their paws under the table? I couldn't believe it when I was welcomed inside and offered a bowl of water. The staff are so efficient and kind. When we entered, the head waiter took trouble to find us a table by the fire where he assumed I would be particularly comfortable. I was. The carpet was lush. As I usually have to make do with flagstone floors this was a real treat.

I was tempted to get up when the duck waddled in. It would have been good to have made contact with this little feathered creature, but this wasn't possible. On spotting the duck Auntie Liz grabbed my lead tight just in case I made a dash towards him.

On the walk, while Auntie Liz and Helen were taking in the landscape and the history of this place, I was enjoying the smells. Having been deprived of a conversation with the duck who tried to enter the hotel bar, I needed some kind of stimulation, which thankfully came in the form of rabbit and fox smells. Delicious. We stopped for a while in the wood; that was fun. Helen called it mysterious and I think I know what she meant. The cricket grounds were rather too well groomed for my liking, far better to stick to the little paths and tracks, following the signposts sometimes, and simply following our noses when we felt like it. I was amused to notice that one gate that we passed bore a notice which stated that if the dog couldn't manage to get over the gate, there was a dog flap fitted at the bottom, but went on to request that walkers close it after use. We did just that, as this gate offered entry to a lovely buttercup field where I could run free. Great fun.

theme park in Michigan. Fortunately, he wasn't permitted to do this and had to make do with a single cottage from the Gloucestershire village of Chedworth instead. William Morris was equally impressed and declared Bibury to be the most beautiful village in the land.

Bibury stands about 12 miles north-west of Cirencester on the B4425. The Swan Hotel stands on the main road through the village, opposite the picturesque bridge that leads to Bibury's famous trout farm.

Dogs are very welcome here. Ducks are not! I mention this because one very persistent little duck had left his companions on the Coln to attempt an entry into the hotel. The main door was open slightly as it was a reasonably warm day, and spotting this, the duck walked arrogantly into the bar, not once but several times. In the end the waiter who had attempted to evict him picked him up, carried him purposefully across the road to the river, and shut the door firmly on his return. That incident amused Pythius immensely as he is familiar with the story of the ugly duckling who turns into a swan.

One of the first things you will notice on entering the hotel is that many of the direction signs are written in both English and Japanese, as Bibury is a popular spot with visiting Orientals.

This enchanting ivy-clad, 17th-century coaching inn offers lunch in its spacious bar area which is lavishly furnished with comfortable green leather chairs and Scottish plaid wall covering. Wood fires add atmosphere. A black grand piano stands in the reception area and, as Liz remarked, the toilets have a real wow factor. In other words, it's a splendid place which welcomes well-behaved dogs, but does suggest that walkers leave muddy boots at the main door.

The lunch menu offers a great selection of moderately priced snacks and hot meals, including platters to share and Bibury trout which is served grilled to perfection. No visitor should leave Bibury without either tasting a trout or taking home a bag of trout from the trout farm. They really are delicious.

The walk

Most walks in Bibury begin by walking the short distance from the Swan to Arlington Row and taking the lane to the right of these picturesque cottages. This lane leads uphill to a junction of signed pathways. If you follow the sign to Ready Token it will take you to a metal gate and a field where you will find several footpath signs. Take the path to the left which is a cart track with a fence on the left until you come to a magnificent stone stile by a field gate. You are walking alongside a wood now and eventually a very well groomed cricket ground. Because there are so many signed footpaths on this walk, the choice really is yours. If your dog just needs a bit of exercise, enjoy the wood, or skirt round the cricket ground. You can now continue along the

track, to cross the river near a mill. You will soon come to Bibury Court, built by Sir Robert Sackville in 1623. A wing was added 16 years later which was designed by Inigo Jones. If you continue, you will come to a road where you turn left then past a junction and left through a gap in the wall when you see a hotel sign. Now you have joined the road back to where you started, having passed the church and the school. Or you can do as we did, and just follow the footpath signs as the fancy takes you. We encountered one corner where there were five footpath signs all pointing in different directions. Following them at whim was such fun and there's no real chance of getting lost as you are climbing uphill slightly; the sight of Bibury with its higgledy-piggledy tiled roofs and mellowing grey stone buildings is never far away. So – a walk around Bibury can last as long as you want it to.

The Perch Inn, Binsey

When you enter the little village of Binsey – half way down Binsey Lane, off the Botley Road, as you approach Oxford from the west – you are entering a beautiful and enchanted place steeped in history. What's more, the transition from a modern-day traffic jam to the tranquil environment of Binsey is almost instant. Having made that left turn down Binsey Lane, you are in deep country within moments. Only the low hum of traffic travelling on the nearby ring road reminds you of the world you have left behind.

Half a mile down the lane you approach the Perch, and may wonder why a pub that dates back to the 17th century looks so pristine and new. This is because it was badly damaged by fire in 2007 but thankfully it was almost completely rebuilt in 2008, much to the delight of the many walkers who use it as a watering hole when circumnavigating Port Meadow.

Some people visit this pub when they want to escape from the city; others call in while walking the River Thames, and others call in for refreshments before carrying on down the lane to the little 12th-century church dedicated to St Margaret of Antion. It's here they can pay homage to St Frideswide, Oxford's patron saint, and see the treacle well which Lewis Carroll immortalised in *Alice's Adventures in Wonderland*.

Frenchman Johnny Mignon, who runs the pub, is a great believer in serving local food. He acquires most of his ingredients from the nearby pick-your-own in Binsey Lane, run by the enterprising Gee family. The farm's close proximity means that Johnny can produce sun-fresh strawberries and freshly harvested fruits and vegetables that are often picked just minutes before they arrive in his kitchen.

Dogs are allowed to sit in the bar area, but must not venture into the restaurant with its starched damask tablecloths and highly polished wine glasses. As Pythius often arrives here after a long river walk, and is often still dripping wet, we sometimes sit in the large garden at the rear when the weather's good, which we can enter via the river towpath. He enjoys sitting in the garden, as many of the Oxford students who also visit this pub tend to make a big fuss of him – well, he is a very handsome dog.

Pythius says

I love Binsey. Because I am a very perceptive dog, I can sense the history associated with this place, and was very sad when I learned that fire had destroyed this lovely old thatched pub. How good it was to discover it was open again and dogs like me were still permitted to place our paws under the table while our owners tucked into a hearty lunch. I don't often get offered a bowl of water here, but that's OK as I have usually drunk my fill while darting in and out of the Thames.

There have been times when I have got myself into big trouble when dashing up and down the river path between the Perch and the Trout. Once I met up with a rather large black and white cow who wouldn't get out of my way. We eventually came to an amicable arrangement, cow and I, she went one way and I went another, but it was a bit fraught for a moment or two. Then there was the time I decided to chase a fisherman's float that was bobbing about in the water. Perhaps the less said about that episode the better. Some things just shouldn't be mentioned. I love this walk when there are no fishermen, as there are little inlets and bays all the way, where I can splash about to my heart's content.

The walk

On leaving the Perch, you can continue along Binsey Lane for about half a mile and visit the church and treacle well. That's a marvellous experience as you are walking in the footsteps of Lewis Carroll who walked this lane with Alice Liddle, his inspiration for the Alice stories. Pythius doesn't think much of that walk as it is hard-surfaced road all the way; he sees it as more of a pilgrimage than a walk.

Leaving our car in the Perch car park, we usually take the Thames towpath from the bottom of the pub's garden, and turn left. It takes approximately half an hour to travel along the towpath from the Perch to the Trout at Godstow, where we often stop for a drink. Dogs are only allowed outside at the Trout, but we don't mind that; we enjoy sitting besides the river with our drinks as we watch the tame peacocks strut around the grounds.

Cross the bridge after leaving the Trout and you can walk back to the Perch through Port Meadow along the other side of the river, providing you respect the fact that there are livestock in the meadow and keep your dog under control. This is a superb walk which brings you to a pair of bridges, which you cross to get back to the Perch (turn right once you are over the river).

One word of warning: You will often encounter cattle along the towpath, and there are horses in the meadow. Fishermen can be a problem too as they frequently hold fishing competitions along the towpath at weekends. They tend to get very cross if they discover you have a water-loving dog disturbing the waters.

It's worth mentioning that Port Meadow, which stretches from Jericho to Wolvercote along the east bank of the Thames, is an ancient area of grazing land which was given to the Freemen of Oxford by King Alfred who founded the city in the 10th century. The Freemen's collective right to graze their animals on the meadow free of charge was recorded in the Domesday Book in 1086. Because this land has never been ploughed it contains well preserved archaeological remains some of which survive as residual earthworks, including Bronze age round barrows.

The King's Head, Bledington

I love phoning the King's Head to book a table, requesting one for two humans and two dogs – the receptionist accepts this arrangement without a murmur. She obviously gets requests like this all the time, judging by the number of dogs and their owners who call in for lunch.

The King's Head was formerly a 16th-century cider house. This becomes obvious as soon as you enter, as it is simply oozes old world charm and character. Set back from the village green, with its pretty little brook that comes complete with a collection of very noisy ducks that patrol the area, it's all very picturesque.

This is a pub Pythius and I visit often with my friend Kate, a volunteer Cotswold Warden, one of more than 340 volunteers who help to keep the Cotswolds special. She has an adorable black Labrador named Polly, who gets on so well with Pythius that we frequently combine a dog walk with a pub lunch.

The King's Head is one of Kate's favourite winter pubs as there's always a blazing log fire in the main bar area. After a long walk on a bitterly cold day, it's a very agreeable sight.

Pythius says

Helen's right, this is a wonderful winter pub. The fire is just what a border collie needs after one of Auntie Kate's long walks. Polly likes it too. And because the pub's owners accept that children and dogs are all part of the family, we are treated with great respect when we visit. A bowl of water is brought to our table and no one seems to mind if we spread ourselves out a bit and make ourselves at home beside the inglenook fireplace.

What Helen has not said about this walk, is that from September to February it's simply swarming with pheasants. They are everywhere. They were in the maize field, in the woods, and some are often lurking in the hedgerows. Obviously, Polly and I are put on our leads when pheasants come into view. Of course, the sight of those delicious birds waddling around defying us to catch them frustrates us. However once we reach the river, our leads are removed and we have the time of our lives. We love the splashy field too. Never have I encountered such a soggy field. Great fun, especially when Auntie Kate and Helen are struggling to stop their Wellingtons getting sucked into the mud. That's always an amusing sight.

High back settles and low beams add to its appeal. Both children and dogs are welcome here. In fact, there's a family dining area behind the main bar which echoes to the sound of youthful laughter during Sunday lunch sessions.

The King's Head never fails to offer the most mouth-watering food which, where possible, is sourced locally. The Aberdeen Angus beef, for example, is reared in a nearby village and slaughtered locally. The fresh bread, which is delivered daily, is baked nearby at Daylesford Organics. The Cheddar cheese comes from Daylesford Organics too, and all the fruit and vegetables come from the nearby village of Oddington and the Vale of Evesham which is known for its fertile soil and abundant harvests.

When possible, Kate and I request a table near the fire. Pythius and Polly know this and make for that area immediately, then spread themselves out and bask in its warmth while we fortify ourselves with a glass or two of real ale.

The King's Head is a free house and there's always a great selection of local brews on tap. In fact, you can taste a different local beer every time you visit. There are some very tasty Gloucestershire ciders on tap too, and the Cotswold lager, which is brewed nearby, is certainly worth trying.

The traditional Sunday lunch is mindblowing. In fact, the first time Kate and I were presented with a plate of this pub's roast beef, we gave out a gasp of delight as it comes freshly carved complete with all the trimmings.

To attempt a long walk after a meal at the King's Head would prove difficult, so we do the walk first, and then bask in the luxury of a warm fire and a lunch to simply die for.

The walk

A sheet of country walks can be picked up in the pub. They include a nine-mile circular walk from Bledington to Nether Westcote, Idbury and Bruern Abbey, which is particularly pastoral. You can also head across country to Chastleton House, one of the finest Jacobean country houses in the country. We chose to take a three-mile walk which allows us to follow the twisting path of the River Evenlode; however, even on a dry day it calls for wellington boots as there are a couple of fields that are really waterlogged.

You begin this walk by taking the road directly opposite the pub, which leads towards Kingham. Don't turn right out of the village but follow the village street (Chapel Street) beside the stream till you get to what was once the post office on the right (it still retains the post box built into the wall), having passed a sign warning you that ducks are crossing the road. Here turn left onto a footpath that begins at College Place (a private house). You will note the footpath sign pinned to the left hand sign of a wooden gate, which is half hidden by foliage. It may take you a moment to work out how to navigate the path at this point without intruding on the residents' privacy. By bearing to the right as you approach the house you will spot the footpath, which leads to a wooden bridge and a large field. Follow the path, which is worn by countless feet which have walked this field, and then the track leads to woodland and passes through a kissing gate. Turn right and be prepared to meet some pretty muddy patches. As this lane begins to bear left, look for a kissing gate on the right, which is sometimes difficult to spot.

Now you have entered a field through which the river Evenlode winds. Keep the river on your left; enjoy its twists and turns as it wriggles its way across several fields. This is where you really do need Wellington boots, so be prepared.

You will eventually come to dry fields and the disused railway line. This is the point where the fields end, leaving you to turn left and cross an attractive little wooden bridge and three different way markers showing the alternative ways of finishing this walk. We take the path on the far right, which leads back into Bledington and the sign warning drivers to be alert for ducks.

The Kingsbridge Inn, Bourton-on-the-Water

Now and again Liz and I enjoy blending in with all the tourists and pretending we are on holiday, even though we have not journeyed far from home. There's no better place to do this than Bourton-on-the-Water, one of the most picturesque villages in England. It's certainly one of the most visited of the Cotswold villages due to the abundance of shops and the many tourist attractions that can be found here. Besides, what other place also boasts a river running parallel to the main street, and consequently, right through the middle of the town?

Bourton-on-the-Water's origins date back to 400 BC, when a Celtic military camp covering more than 60 acres existed to the north-east of the present village. The Romans took over this camp for a while and the Saxons used it too, changing its name to Salmonsbury. Having gained the status of Site of Special Scientific Interest, Salmonsbury is now in the capable hands of the Gloucestershire Wildlife Trust. It's here that visitors can enjoy walking through hay meadows that support an abundance of different species, including early marsh orchids and quaking grass. The meandering River Eye also flows through this reserve. As

Pythius says

I'm not sure I go a bundle on all this tourist stuff – too many people – not enough natural smells. But Helen and Auntie Liz seem to enjoy it now and again, so who am I to argue if they take me into a very busy pub and insist I behave myself? All I can remember about this pub is feet, loads of feet, some wearing sandals, some wearing boots and some with flip-flops or no shoes on at all. But that's what you see when you are a dog sitting under the table in a busy pub in the heart of a tourist centre. I coped of course, particularly when an elderly couple on a nearby table noted my presence and made nice comments about my shiny fur and sparkling eyes.

On the walk, when we came to the end of that little lane and into that glorious meadow, I knew that Auntie Liz and Helen had got it right. What a wonderful river the Windrush is, I love it. Because it manoeuvres its way over pebbles, there's no mud, just lovely crisp, clean water, which tastes as good as it looks. I make that remark because I wasn't offered a bowl of water at the pub and neither Auntie Liz or Helen thought to ask for one. I think they were so bemused by all the bric-a-brac hanging about the place they forgot my needs. Anyway, the walk was great, though perhaps it's best to call it an amble. I would have liked to have stayed there all day, but we eventually moved on to the Model Village.

I assumed that I would miss out on this tourist attraction, but the man on the gate was so impressed by my good behaviour that he let me go in for just a moment, providing Helen kept me on a short lead. Well, he was just closing down for the night and there were no other visitors about. Oh what fun that was. Can you imagine how it feels for a dog who normally only sees feet, to suddenly find himself elevated to roof level and able to look over the chimney pots of little houses and gaze down on miniature trees? Resisting the urge to dip my paws into the miniature river, I walked round with great care loving every moment that I was allowed to walk so tall.

this little river supports one of the country's remaining populations of water vole, and since otters and barns owls are known to frequent this area, it's a very special place indeed.

Unfortunately there's no parking available next to or on the reserve, but visitors can leave their car at a pay and display car park on Station Road and access the site via Greystones Lane. So if you are looking for both history and natural history there's plenty here.

Most visitors head for the centre of the village for lunch, making for the Kingsbridge Inn, a colourful pub decorated with masses of hanging baskets, which stands besides the River Windrush. This is one of those pubs that cater for every conceivable kind of visitor. Children are welcome and can select meals from a menu written specially for them, pensioners are able to select from a 'two-for-one' deal, and those in between can enjoy a range of fine ales and a menu which is so comprehensive, virtually everyone is catered for. Yes – dogs are welcome too providing they keep their paws well under the table.

When you first enter the Kingsbridge Inn, you will find it's quite dark. Your eyes may need time to adjust. Once focused, you will encounter so many pictures, mirrors, ornaments, fruit machines and bric-a-brac scattered around that you won't know where to look first. Even one of the lower beams is cluttered with jugs and ornaments.

Because it is a very busy pub, customers are required to obey certain rules, like standing in the right place to order their food and remembering to pick up their cutlery before sitting down. However, food (which is cheap and cheerful) arrives rapidly and is always served with a smile. Although a sign outside boasts that home-cooked food is served here, the items listed on the menu suggests that the chefs occasionally has recourse to the freezer; however, the portions are generous and it tastes fine, and all part of the tourist experience.

The walk

Because Pythius was looking rather anxious when we left the Kingsbridge Inn, Liz and I decided to take him to the back streets and find a walk that took us away from the crowds. As it happened, we found the most delightful walk just by chance by taking a left-hand turn off the High Street into Sherborne Street. It was here that we discovered a sign for The Windrush Way, close to the Duke of Wellington pub. After walking down a little lane as the sign directed, we found ourselves in a beautiful meadow abutting the river, which seemed so far away from the crowds we could have been in the middle of open country. Pythius was delighted, rushed to the river and on discovering it wasn't very deep immediately began his 'splashing about in the river' dance, which at times is quite spectacular, with water going in every direction as he thrashes his paws about. That always makes us laugh.

This walk is not long; we followed the footpath for about half a mile keeping pace with the river's gentle movements, until we came to buildings and a lane, which would have taken us back to the main town. At this point we turned and ambled back the way we had come, taking our time, stopping every now and again to sit besides the river while Pythius continued his dance. On finishing the walk Liz and I declared we were refreshed and ready to do the tourist thing again and so headed for one of Bourton-on-the-Water's most famous visitor attractions – the Model Village – which stands behind the Old New Inn, Rissington Road. Built from local stone and slate it's an exact scaled down copy of the town as it was in the 1930s. It never fails to delight.

The Crown and Trumpet, Broadway

Broadway is often referred to as the Jewel in the Cotswolds. Those who visit this picturesque town with its honey-coloured limestone buildings soon discover why. It lies beneath the northern slopes of the Cotswold escarpment on the edge of the Vale of Evesham in one of the most beautiful parts of the Cotswolds. You reach it on the A44, which bypasses the town. It stands midway between Moreton-in-Marsh and Evesham.On this trip we were lucky enough to have been driven there by Pythius' friend, Uncle John.

Broadway was originally a busy stagecoach stop on the route from Worcester to London. Now it's a popular tourist stop, and a centre for arts and antiques. This area attracts a great number of walkers too.

If you park your car in the public car park off Church Street, you can't miss the Crown and Trumpet, a 17th-century inn a couple of minutes' walk away.

I was recommended to try this lovely old pub by a member of CAMRA, as it serves a great selection of real ales, which are kept in perfect condition. You will find the Crown and Trumpet listed in most beer and pub guides and for good reason. This is one of those delightfully friendly pubs that manages to keep its atmosphere local even though it also attracts tourists looking for the traditional English inn which oozes old-world atmosphere.

No one is disappointed when they order a pint of best bitter here, particularly if they try the Wizard's Brew. This beer is brewed especially for the Crown and Trumpet by Stanway, the local brewery, which is situated in a manor house built during the reign of Elizabeth I. Stanway is one of only two log-fired breweries in the country, which makes it particularly special, and its beer particularly tasty.

The food at the Crown and Trumpet is good too, as it's all prepared and cooked on the premises using both local produce and, where possible, local recipes. The Worcester pie of minced beef flavoured with Worcester sauce and the Evesham bubble and squeak are certainly worth ordering. So are the faggots, made by a local butcher – and all at very modest prices.

When I asked if Pythius was able to join us for lunch I was told that providing I tucked him away under the table he would be more than welcome, and he was. Once Uncle John and I were happily settled with our drinks, the licensee came over and congratulated us on having such

---

Pythius says

I admit to being dog tired by the time I had got my paws under the table of this pub. It proved such a cosy, comfortable place that curling up and falling asleep was easy. Whilst I remember hearing children laughing in the background and the sound of plates being cleared from tables, I don't remember much else. I guess that says a great deal about this pub, which was one of those places where I felt secure and snug immediately. I had no need to remain on dog-duty while Helen and Uncle John enjoyed their meal, so I slept. Well why not, we'd had a great walk – I was dog tired.

What Helen has not told you is that the wooden stiles along the way (of which there are many) are particularly dog-friendly. I mention this because when we got to one at the end of the woods she and Uncle John went into a bit of a panic. 'How can we get Pythius through?'asked Uncle John as he inspected the netting surrounding the stile and noted there was no dog-hole.

'Oh he can jump it if we help him,' Helen replied, but she didn't look very confident. Indeed she was about to remove her coat and hang it on the stile so that I could see clearly just what it was I had to jump.

I just stood there, my eyes focusing on what was clearly a clever little wooden dog flap to the right of the stile, that could be lifted to allow us dogs through. It was simply ages before they realised exactly what it was I'd noticed. Within seconds of following my gaze however, the flap was opened up and I trotted through feeling rather smug. It's not often I get a chance to show them just how intelligent I am. All the way back Uncle John kept muttering things about me being smarter than they were. There were several of these stiles, each one designed slightly differently, but each offering an easy way for dogs to continue the walk, once their masters had worked out what to do.

a lovely dog. He went on to explain that well behaved dogs such as Pythius were always welcome, but added that not all dogs calling in knew how to behave.

Pythius was so exhausted from our four-mile walk to Buckland and back that he didn't even lift his head to acknowledge this compliment. He clearly felt very comfortable here. Children are also welcome at this pub which has a special children's menu.

The walk

We could have taken the walk to the Broadway Tower on its hilltop site in the Broadway Country Park, but chose to walk to the pretty little village of Buckland instead. We were looking for a gentle amble rather than a strenuous climb to the summit of the second highest point in the wolds.

Our walk, which took us about two hours to complete, began by turning left out of the High Street car park and into Church Street. Once we had passed the 19th-century church, St Michaels and All Angels, we crossed the road into West End Lane, following a wooden footpath sign for the Cotswold Way. This took us into a large field filled with a large flock of very docile sheep, with pretty black faces.

Because this walk is very popular, it's virtually impossible to get lost as countless footsteps have marked the way through the field, across a small wooden bridge that takes you over a stream and into another large field. This field had no livestock in it when we walked. Be careful now, because you will soon come to a stile which leads to a small tarmac road. Dogs should be put on the lead now, but on crossing the road and approaching the Broadway Coppice they can be allowed their freedom again, This is a fascinating wood that dances with bluebells during the spring.

There are way markers all along the path through the woods, so there's no fear of getting lost. Unfortunately the path was rather muddy in parts when we took this route, but we coped, though at times it was with some difficulty.

When you leave the woods you will find the path winds round and towards Buckland, until you come to a point where you are requested to keep your dog on a lead as you walk a small enclosed pathway past private gardens. Once you have reached the main road that runs through the village, turn right past St Michael's churchand then right again at a green footpath marker which will link you to the route you left.

Before leaving Buckland you might like to stop off and visit the Church (photo right), which is mostly 13th and 14th century and houses some really lovely old Jacobean pews.

Those who find climbing stiles awkward may be in difficulties during this walk, as the stiles come thick and fast, particularly when you reach the coppice. However, the views this walk offers are simply breathtaking, for although you are climbing quite a steep slope during the first part of the walk, it's well worth the effort when you get to the top and are presented with a stunning panoramic view of the surrounding countryside.

The Lamb Inn, Burford

The Lamb simply has to be included in this collection, for not only is it an exceptionally dog-friendly pub but I have a personal connection with it too. My grandfather was the Burford blacksmith and metal worker and my father was therefore brought up amidst the trappings of a blacksmith's forge. He spent much of his youth helping his father repair milk churns, and forge everyday items out of metal. Apparently, the first thing he ever made was a suit of armour for his teddy bear! One of the next things he made was the metal inn sign that continues to hang outside The Lamb Inn.

Every time I pass this sign I am reminded of my roots in this charming Cotswold town, so naturally I always call at the Lamb when I'm in Burford.

Burford lies in the valley of the Windrush River. If you enter the town from the A40, you will drive down the hill, passing the stumpy willows on both side of the street and then encounter its picturesque heart made up of a jumbled juxtaposition of gabled houses, privately-owned shops, pubs and restaurants, with their lichen-encrusted roofs.

There have been times when national companies, who have made their mark on other High Streets, have attempted to infiltrate this ancient Cotswold town, but to no avail. Strangely they never succeed. Those who know and love Burford say the force of local opinion will never let them in.

The Lamb was originally built out of local stone as a weaver's cottage in 1420. The moment you step through the main door of this wisteria-clad building and spot its worn flagstone floor, you are aware that you are stepping into Cotswold history. I always ask myself as I enter, how many footsteps have passed this way to give these flagstones such a worn and polished look? It's a question that has no answer – who can ever tell just how many pints have been poured here or how many artisans have walked into this pub at the end of a busy day? I would like to think that my grandfather and his father before him leaned against this bar enjoying a pint or two.

A welcome is certainly assured for both myself and Pythius when we call. He's usually asked if he would like a drink before my half pint has been poured. It comes in a bowl marked DOG and is gently placed besides him, even during busy times. During the winter months, you can enjoy a glass of warm mulled wine in the intimate little bar area, while sitting besides a roaring log fire.

Fish features large on the bar menu, so it is always worth inquiring about the fish dish of the day. You will not be disappointed. Fresh local produce is also cooked here where possible and all dishes are cooked to order. In the winter, a bowl of the Lamb's home-made soup is certainly worth trying, especially after a long walk, although I must admit that the fish and chips served here is second to none.

The walk

There are lots of great walks starting from Burford. The Tourist Information Centre, Sheep Street, has a local walks leaflet. The first, which is just a mile and a half, takes you to Westhall Hill. It begins at the bottom of the High Street, and over the bridge, turning right at the mini roundabout up the A361 for 600 yards; then make a left hand turn which will take you to the 16th-century manor house. By taking a foot-path just before the manor house, you can follow footpath signs which will take you back to Burford Bridge.

When we walk with Uncle John, we do something far more adventurous. We meet up in Burford's official car park and on leaving one car there, we drive to Little Barrington, parking the car in front of the Village Hall and walk back to Burford. As this walk ends at Sheep Street, and the Lamb is the first pub we encounter, this three-mile walk is perfect, providing we don't mind juggling with the cars afterwards. You can turn this into a circular walk, but as that is six and a half miles long, it's for those who want to really stride out.

Once parked at Great Barrington village hall car park, you will spot a way-marker taking you on part of D'Arcy Dalton Way, which is a 66 mile-long path created in 1986 by the Oxford Fieldpaths Society. If you stick to this route you will end up on the Wessex Downs. But we don't!

Pythius says

Helen gets very excited when we approach the Lamb. She always points to the inn sign, forgetting she has already told me that her father made it during his youth. I try to absorb this information as if for the first time – such things keep her happy.

I must say that this really is a dog-friendly pub, and I am usually served before her, which is nice, especially if we have been on one of those long walks that Uncle John from Witney organises for us.

In the winter there are lovely log fires glowing away in this pub, just the thing a dog like me needs if I have spent time splashing about in the Windrush by the car park. Helen always parks in the official free car park when visiting Burford, as she finds that reversing in and out of the car spaces along the main street is far too difficult. You will find the car park signposted to the right as you reach the bottom of the High Street.

I wasn't too sure that a walk which would require me to pad down a country road for more than two miles would be much fun. Yet it was. I really do enjoy the views. I loved the first two fields we passed through too. They were big and grassy and as there were no livestock in them, I was able to run and run to my heart's delight. Large cow pats in the middle of these fields suggest they are occupied by bovine creatures from time to time. A sign warning walkers that dogs found worrying the livestock could be shot, concerned me somewhat.

After leaving the fields we came to a really muddy lane, which seemed to cause Helen and Uncle John a bit of a problem, but I managed it perfectly by darting through the fence, so that I could run on grass until we got to the end. That was the moment when a fluffy dog darted out of the Church Farm Cottages. He proved a bit of a pain, far too familiar for my liking, but once I'd shaken him off it was uphill all the way. Then back to the glorious Lamb Inn.

This path will take you over a couple of fields on a very muddy path leading to Barrington Mill, then on to Church Farm, where you cross an old wooden bridge over the River Windrush. Turn left and you will come to Middle Road.

At this junction we turned right for a moment to view St Peter's Church, which dates back to Norman times and is well worth a visit, then turned back and walked towards Burford.

I admit being alarmed on discovering that two-and-a-half miles of this walk would be on road. But after walking it, I changed my mind. Never have I encountered such a tranquil path, which has views to die for. We did encounter one car as we walked, but it was travelling at a reasonable speed and immediately made provisions for us to pass it safely. It's the views on the left hand side that make this walk so enchanting. Rolling landscape and the

meandering River Windrush create a spellbinding landscape that simply can't be beaten. Even Pythius stopped from time to time to check the view. Vast amounts of horse droppings along this road suggested that we might encounter horses too. We didn't, although we did pass several dog walkers and an enthusiastic rambler from Germany who had already travelled 12 miles and was about to walk a further four.

There are no further instructions needed, you just follow this rural country road until you reach a junction. Turn left at this point, keeping to the footpath beside the road, and you will eventually come to Sheep Street and the Lamb Inn, having passed several wooden seats that invite exhausted walkers to sit for a moment or two. At this point, a delicious pint awaits you.

The Tite Inn, Chadlington

Chadlington is an ancient village that dates back to the time of the Domesday Book. It lies midway between Burford and Chipping Norton. Although its population is little more than 2,000, this remarkable village boasts a fine church, an amazingly well-stocked village shop and a charming 17th-century pub situated on the outskirts of the village at Mill End.

There's a blue signpost pointing to the pub, but during the spring and summer months the leaves of overhanging branches obscure it slightly. You may have to double back if you miss the turn.

No one is sure how the Tite got its name, but presumably this was where villagers once collected their water. It has been serving the local community as a pub for more than 200 years and remains a popular drinking place.

The Tite underwent a massive refurbishment in 2007, reopening in February 2008, much to the delight of the locals and the many visitors from outlying areas who are drawn to Chadlington's village shop. This

---

Pythius says

Well, I'd give this pub ten tail wags out of ten if I hadn't been inspected by the resident pooch who arrogantly marched over to our table the moment I'd got settled. What's a chap to think if his unmentionables are inspected just as he's got his paws under the table? Fortunately the kindly landlady noticed my discomfort and ordered him out immediately, then returned to our table with a large bowl of iced water especially for me. That was nice.

The walk was perfect. A little brook follows the path all the way along, which simply begs to be sampled, and a couple of meadows filled with buttercups, where I could dry myself off with a quick run, provided even more exercise. What more could a dog ask for? Perfect, simply perfect.

Helen and Auntie Liz stopped every so often to admire the view while I splashed and paddled about in the brook. They laughed when I jumped out of the brook and then ran round and round in the meadow and ended up covered with yellow petals. Whilst Helen and Auntie Liz only walked about a mile each way, I certainly covered far more miles than that. I was definitely exhausted by the time we got back to the car.

remarkable shop has served the village for many years, but began to suffer bad times at the end of the 20th century. When it was threatened with closure in 2001, villagers rallied round and clubbed together to buy non-profit shares to get it going again. It has flourished ever since as it not only stocks an outstanding selection of world-class cheeses, local produce and home-made cakes, but shares the premises with a popular butchers shop too.

Since the new owners moved into the Tite, slate flagstones and polished wooden floors have replaced the floral-patterned carpet that once ran through the three small rooms. Exposed beams, original Cotswold stone walls and two large fireplaces give it a rustic look and old settles and an assortment of wooden tables and chairs do the rest.

Dogs are certainly welcome here if they stay in the bar area and not the two small dining rooms, which stand either side of the bar.

Local produce dominates both the lunch and dinner menus and all dishes are cooked from scratch on the premises. Portions are generous and prices reasonable. If you enjoy home-made beefburgers created from local beef, this is the pub for you. They do a great beef provençal too. As a free house, the Tite provides an interesting assortment of real ales, many coming from the Purity Brewing Company which only supplies pubs situated within a 50-mile radius of their brewery in Warwickshire.

The walk

The walk couldn't be closer; it begins at the gate opposite the pub. As the Tite's car park is extensive, we were allowed to keep our car there whilst we explored the countryside. There are several walks that begin in the vicinity – this is the sort of area where you can walk as far as you like and still discover there are more footpaths ahead. However, we chose this path as we'd been told it's particularly beautiful in the spring, as it is. May blossom hangs heavy throughout the walk. A profusion of buttercups add colour to the scene. It begins as an ancient green lane that wanders so far from a main road you would be able to hear the silence if it wasn't for the gurgling waters of the little babbling brook that follows the lane. By taking this path which bears right after about a quarter of a mile, passing through several very stylish wooden gates installed by volunteer Cotswold wardens, you will end up at Brookend which is the other side of the village. We could have turned it into a circular walk by returning via the village, but as the scenery was so beautiful and Pythius was having such fun splashing about in the water, we ambled back the way we had come. We probably only walked about a mile in total, but it took us at least an hour as we took our time and kept stopping to enjoy this lovely unspoiled footpath.

Apparently this path can become very overgrown during the summer months and there is a particularly damp rather muddy patch half way along.

The Bell Hotel, Charlbury

One of the great things about the charming Cotswold town of Charlbury, perched high above the east bank of the River Evenlode, is its railway station and regular bus services. Easy access to public transport means visitors can stay for the day or the weekend without travelling by car. It also means residents can commute with ease from its Brunelian station to Oxford – or even London, which can be reached in just one hour ten minutes.

Charlbury is six miles from Chipping Norton and seven miles from Woodstock, and whichever way you approach it, you will find yourself travelling through the most beautiful unspoiled countryside and woodlands. Perhaps the most striking thing about Charlbury is its close proximity to Wychwood Forest. What remains of this ancient forest is one of the commanding features of the Evenlode Valley in which Charlbury sits. And with an ancient forest comes a rich diversity of wildlife and species-rich hedgerows which will delight walkers who venture forth after a delicious pub lunch at the Bell.

This 18th-century hotel stands in Church Street, the very heart of Charlbury. Its large car park and spacious garden at the rear with a charming little stream at the bottom is a bonus, especially on a summer day as the Bell prides itself on serving picnic hampers for those who want to eat al fresco. The interior is broken up into several small rooms, all stylishly decorated to reflect both the age of the building and modern trends. One of these intimate spaces is covered with gilt-edged mirrors that look simply stunning as they are hung close together for greater impact.

Pythius and I always walk into the Bell with confidence, as dogs are allowed in unreservedly. Water is often offered to Pythius before my own order is taken. He likes that.

Cask marque ales on tap offer the drinker a great choice and the local produce used in the kitchen makes a very positive contribution to the meals served here, which are all cooked from scratch. It's always worth looking at the specials menu if taking lunch, as it often offers some very imaginative dishes and all at a very reasonable price. The freshly cut doorstep sandwiches are worth ordering too if you are really hungry. And because the owners of this friendly establishment are passionate about sourcing local seasonal produce, the food served here can be taken seriously.

The walk

As the Oxfordshire Way runs through the town, a considerable number of rewarding walks can be taken from here. You can follow the Evenlode valley to Chadlington, or walk east to Ditchley. The more energetic can also take an 8-mile circular walk beside Cornbury Park and through Wychwood Forest; or explore the Oxfordshire Way (Stonesfield is 3 miles away and Woodstock and Blenheim Park 6 miles). Before embarking on our walk, we called into Charlbury's charming little bookshop, which sells a great selection of books of local interest and maps.

We were warned that we would probably encounter livestock and horses on the northern route of the Oxfordshire Way and suggested we went for a shorter, but no less picturesque circular walk.

The path leading to this walk is on the right as you walk down Dyers Hill towards the station, a few yards before you cross the river. It is signposted Mill Field, Watery Lane and Pound Hill; however, above this green sign is a large white sign which states that Mill Lane is a private road. On

Pythius says

Yes, I do like the Bell, particularly when Helen lets me splash around a bit in the little stream at the bottom of the garden after lunch. I am always allowed to sit wherever I want, which is nice, and so I tend to trot into the small dinning area in the room opposite the main bar, as it has lovely wooden floors that are firm but comfortable to lie on. When a log fire is burning brightly in the fireplace, it's even better. A bowl of water is always served under the table very promptly. As Helen remarked, I usually get served before she does, not that she minds, of course. The sooner I settle down, the sooner she and Auntie

Liz can relax. They do tend to fret when I turn round and round in order to get myself really comfortable, but I am a dog and that's what dogs do.

I admit to getting into a real grump on the walk when Auntie Liz and Helen refused to join me in the flood water that filled Watery Lane. After all what did they expect from a lane with that name? There are times when they are real wimps. Starting this walk from Mill Lane didn't seem too promising at first, particularly as they insisted I remain on my lead – then hey presto – there it was, the most glorious meadow I have ever seen. Green, lush and wonderful. How quickly life can change when you are a border collie. One moment you are tied to a lead and appearing to go nowhere very interesting at all, then suddenly all those things I dream of lay before me, including not one, but two rivers!

I was able to run from one river to the other, never daring to go in as the water was moving quickly and appeared rather deep (I'm told that dogs less careful than me have fallen in here: you have been warned!), but I enjoyed myself nevertheless. Besides I did find a shallow part half way up where I was able to splash about a bit.

I didn't like that metal bridge at the end of the meadow. Very difficult to walk over – but I did persevere, only to find that within moments of getting to the other side and beginning to enjoy myself again, Helen and Auntie Liz insisted we walk back the way we'd come. That's life, I guess.

seeing this we actually walked past: only on turning and facing the sign full on do you discover this is indeed the entrance to Mill Field. This lane, with houses either side, suddenly opens up as you approach an old sluice gate, a small wooden bridge and kissing gate. Walk through this gate and you will find yourself in the most glorious water meadow with the mill stream on your right and the Evenlode on your left. Amble on for about half a mile, going from one section of the water meadow to the next, passing a wooden memorial seat to W D Campbell on the left, which is now badly in need of repair, and a large stone marker for Campbell's Copse.

W D Campbell was a Charlbury resident who made his mark as a school teacher and naturalist with a gift for sharing his intimate knowledge of the history, language, flora and fauna of Wychwood Forest. His Country Diary column published in *The Guardian* for 30 years was known to thousands, which means his memorial seat is well deserved and should be repaired as befits his memory.

This is not a walk to be hurried. Enjoy the ancient twisted trees, the many wild flowers that grow here in abundance and spend a moment listening to the bird song. Yes, this is the English countryside at its loveliest, especially as you have water flowing on either side as you walk.

You will eventually reach the point where the Evenlode and its mill stream diverge. A metal bridge takes you onto the next part of the walk. Cross it and turn left and you can join the Oxfordshire Way (towards Chadlington and the Wychwoods), but we didn't do that.

After crossing the bridge we turned right again and continued our walk down Watery Lane, which takes you to the foot of Pound Hill and the B4026 which leads back to the centre of Charlbury.

Unfortunately, on the day we walked this way we soon discovered that Watery Lane was not just waterlogged but completely flooded. Naturally Pythius thought this was absolutely wonderful and wondered why we wouldn't follow him as he splashed his way through the water. We aborted that attempt, and walked back the way we had come which, given the beauty of the meadows, was certainly not a hardship.

The Eight Bells,
Chipping Campden

Chipping Campden is one of those Cotswold gems capable of taking your breath away – it's one of the finest of the Cotswold wool towns. This soon becomes evident when you walk down the High Street and observe all the rich 17th-century merchants' houses that are there in abundance. Actually it is so beautiful that wealthy entrepreneurs have made offers to buy parts of it so that the picturesque buildings created from honey-coloured limestone can be dismantled and transported to America and be re-assembled over there.

Similar offers were made for the old London Bridge, which was eventually transported bit by bit to Arizona. However, thankfully the ancient buildings of Chipping Campden – many of which date back to the Middle Ages – are not going anywhere.

Chipping Campden stands on the edge of the Cotswolds in a gentle valley set amid rolling hills and the lush pastures that typify this part of the country. Leaving the A44 just three miles east of Broadway and follow the B4081 into Chipping Campden.

You will find the Eight Bells in Church Street, a side street in the centre of town, which as its name suggests leads you to Chipping Campden's magnificent church, St James, that dates back in parts to the 12th century.

As this pub was built in the 14th century to accommodate the stonemasons who were working on the church, it rates as the oldest surviving public house in town. It gets its name from the fact it was used to store the bells for the church tower while it was being built.

When you first walk into this glorious little pub your eyes may take a moment to adjust to the dark, but this only takes a second or two.. Soon you will be admiring the exposed stone walls and gnarled beams. If you arrive during the winter, you will be thrilled to see that roaring log fires offer an appropriate welcome too.

Dogs are welcome in the bar area and water is provided for your canine friend on request. However, to our surprise, a bowl of water was placed besides Pythius without us having to ask for one.

During our visit we went for a couple of glasses of cloudy scrumpy

Pythius says

No one seemed to take much notice of me during our visit. I simply tucked myself under the table and stayed there until Helen and Auntie Liz had finished their lunch. At some point a waitress placed a large bowl of water besides me, which was very kind of her. What a shame I didn't notice this and tipped it all over the floor when I turned over!

It's a good job I am allowed to have my say when it comes to describing the walks, because there are times when Helen overlooks the funny bits. What she has failed to explain is that we almost got flattened by a herd of sheep rampaging down the hill.

There we were, Helen, Auntie Liz and me, all enjoying a bit of a rest, having clambered down the hill by the car park to a flat grassy field. They were both congratulating themselves on having found such an ideal place to rest. Helen was playing with her camera and Auntie Liz was reading the map – all very idyllic until we heard a bleating noise, which got louder and louder and louder. There they were, hundreds of sheep, the very ones we had seen in an enclosure at the top of the hill earlier on.

They had obviously been shut up for too long, because they were hell bent to get to lower land and freedom. The fact that we were in the way didn't seem to matter. So there we were – one moment at peace with our world, the next grabbing rucksacks and the camera as we desperately tried to get out of the way.

Actually, we made it (well sort of), but it was a real panic moment, particularly as I was not on a lead, and they were concerned I might join the sheep on their lunge for freedom.

I didn't. Actually I acted with great responsibility. Having made sure they were OK, I headed for some trees and a small wood. Auntie Liz and Helen finally caught up with me, and we waited there among the trees while the sheep settled down.

I thought it was great fun, but the fact that Helen failed to mention the incident suggests they didn't. Such is life!

cider which was absolutely delicious, but a wide range of real ales is on tap too. The menu offers a great choice, with all the standard favourites such as fish and chips and more exotic dishes such as home-cooked mushroom and leek risotto. And if you are into puddings – don't leave before trying one: they are lush.

The walk

Should you wish for something different, you could go on the Chipping Campden Sundial Safari. This walk takes you from the scratch dials of the 14th century, past the 19th-century sundial at Grevel's House in the High Street, and on to sundials designed in the 1930s by members of the Arts and Crafts Movement founded by William Morris. But this kind of walk doesn't satisfy a dog such as Pythius who enjoys running free and exploring the countryside.

We did walk the little fellow along the High Street, as we couldn't resist doing a spot of sightseeing. We soon realised, however, that he was not happy about stopping here and there to look in shop windows or admire the ancient architecture just because we had insisted that virtually every building in this street is worth looking at. Dogs aren't into architecture, so we made for Dover's Hill, named after Robert Dover, the founder of the Cotswold Olimpicks (not the Olympic Games!) which are thought to have first taken place in 1612, though some suggest they may have begun even earlier.

Those first Olimpicks included horse racing, hare-coursing, wrestling and staff fighting. Today's festivities, which take place annually on the Friday after Spring Bank Holiday, are more like a cross between pantomime and carnival.

To get to Dover's Hill, we walked south-west along the High Street, turning right into West End Terrace and then Hoo Lane. We carried on along the track, past a farm and then into a field that led us to Kingcomb Lane. It's really easy after that thanks to the countless walkers who have walked left along the escarpment and navigated this path which leads to the top of Dover's Hill.

The view is breathtaking. Some say you can see seven counties on a clear day. You can certainly enjoy a fantastic view of the Vale of Evesham, the plains of the River Avon and the River Severn and even the foothills of Wales on a good day.

We stopped at the parking area, admired the panoramic view and delighted in the fact we were able to take in more than 60 miles of scenery. Then having allowed Pythius to play for a while on the lower ground, we returned the way we had come.

The Chequers, Chipping Norton

The Chequers stands at the junction of Goddards Lane and Market Street, in the middle of the historic town of Chipping Norton. Whilst Chipping Norton has remained a rural town since it was founded in Saxon times, it's famed for an 18th-century resident, the Reverend Edward Stone, who is credited with the discovery of aspirin. A blue plaque honouring his discovery can be found in West Street. Parking is available in the centre of town, but there are two free public car parks close by if this area is too congested.

On walking into the Chequers, you will find yourself facing a series of cosy interlocking rooms in which to sit. The small rooms to the left (one of which has a roaring log fire during the winter months) are where Pythius is always welcome.

It's a Fuller's pub so you can order Chiswick Bitter, London Pride or ESB if you fancy a glass of real ale. Pythius' drink arrives in a plastic tub on which the words 'For a thirsty dog' are written. He's always very impressed by that.

The furniture is chunky and comfortable, colourful rugs adorn the flagstone and pinewood floors, and many pictures and photographs fill the walls. All in all, it has great character, as it should. This pub dates back to the 15th century, although there has been a building on this site since the 12th century.

It was refurbished in 1991 when the courtyard was converted into a restaurant where dogs are not allowed. Pythius doesn't mind at all, he likes the small intimate rooms in which he's welcome.

The menu changes frequently and offers some great curries and home-made steak and kidney pies. Sandwiches are available too. As this pub is but a stone's throw from Chipping Norton's award-winning little theatre, it is often busy just before the curtain goes up as it's a great place to eat before a night out.

Pythius says

I am not happy about beginning a walk in a town; there are too many cars and people. However this pub is so dog-friendly I accept that Chipping Norton is a great place to visit.

I did this walk in the company of my black Labrador friend Polly and her mistress Kate, the Cotswold Warden who walks at a fair pace. Whenever Kate organises a walk, I know that Polly and I are in for a really good time. She strides out with purpose and never gets us lost as she knows the area like the back of her hand. It's good to be in the company of someone like Kate who really knows what they are doing and where they are going.

I just wish she could do something about the mud. There was so much mud on the path at the beginning of this walk when we linked up with the River Cleeves, that there were times Helen had to hang on to Kate lest she should fall. (Something to do with her poorly hip – but we don't talk about that!)

Unfortunately the river is fenced off, except for one small part where I managed to get a bit of a paddle. But there were plenty of places I could run and play, so all in all, this is a very nice walk for dogs. In fact, we passed several other dogs along the way who were also enjoying themselves.

The walk

If you have left your car in the public car park off the A44, simply cross over the road, walk down the hill for 100 yards and take Diston's Lane towards St Mary's Church. This leads you to a kissing gate and a wooded footpath, where you can take your dog off the lead. You will soon find yourself walking alongside the River Cleeves which flows on your right hand side. As it's only a small river you could be forgiven for assuming it's a stream.

You cross the river when you go under the old brick bridge and leave the woods via another kissing gate. Continue along the edge of an open meadow until you get to the next kissing gate.

Be careful now as you are approaching a small tarmac road, and you need to put the dog on the lead. Turn left on reaching this road and walk up the slope towards the attractive little village of Upper Norton.

On seeing the first houses in Upper Norton at Cleeves Corner, leave

the road and turn left into a narrower track where tarmac turns to gravel. From this point it's a matter of following the track which takes you to a high point where you can view Chipping Norton in its entirety. On a clear sunny day this is a beautiful sight.

Carry on and you will reach a junction with a track on the left. At this point you will see various way-markers, including a blue circular sign marked with a footstep which says 'Step into the Cotswolds'. This indicates that the walk is one of many linked with a visitor 'pay back' scheme funded by visitors who make voluntary donations to local access conservation projects, in partnership with West Oxfordshire District Council, and supported by Oxfordshire County Council's Countryside Services. In other words, people care for this area and you are in safe hands.

Take this left hand track and it will lead you back to Chipping Norton, past the church and up the hill to the Chequers. The journey takes under an hour and is easy walking when it's not muddy.

The Hand and Shears, Church Hanborough

The Hand and Shears stands opposite the church of St Peter and St Paul in Church Hanborough, a small village recorded in the Domesday Book. You will find it midway between Witney and Woodstock. You can't miss the village, just look out for the church's soaring spire that pierces the horizon for miles around. It's quite spectacular.

The Hand and Shears has had a chequered career. There have been times when it's proved the most popular pub in the area and others when it has failed to please. At the moment it serves a very decent pub meal and has a warm comfortable atmosphere. The massive fireplace in the main bar area is usually roaring away during the winter months and in the summer a light airy conservatory area offers extra space and a chance to enjoy sunshine filtering through the glass.

The one thing that has stood firm throughout the many changes is

the fact that dogs are always welcome. Pythius loves this pub because he knows a great walk is imminent when we lunch here. The footpath leading to the ancient Pinsey Wood, a country wildlife site, runs besides this pub, so it's an ideal place to begin a magical walk through the woods.

The walk

Pinsley Wood is an ancient remnant of Wychwood Forest which bore the name Pins Wood

Pythius says

I have accompanied Helen into this pub many times. Even though loads of different people have welcomed us over the years, they all seem to enjoy my company. In the winter I am allowed to roast myself by the fire which is nice. In the summer we often sit outside the main door and watch the world go by.

I am instantly aware that this is an ancient wood when we enter. It has a strange earthy kind of smell that has accumulated over the centuries. I find this smell particularly powerful and aromatic during the autumn months when leaves begin falling and the earth is moist. Dogs can detect such things. Well, I certainly can.

I'm allowed to walk without a lead, but Helen never lets me run far, she keeps me quite close to her side at all times. We have seen lots of wildlife when walking this wood, particularly little muntjak deer. Naturally I am tempted to chase them, but manage to restrain myself, because they are indeed very beautiful. Helen seems to respect me for that. In fact, there was a moment during one visit last spring when a muntjak came quite close. Helen spotted it first and called me to heel. We both stood very still so that it wasn't disturbed and could continue grazing. Then suddenly it looked up, saw us staring and fled, jumping through the undergrowth with a lightness of touch I envied somewhat.

in the 13th century. During 2008 it was under threat, when a Kent-based company applied to convert some of this ancient woodland into a sporting centre. Fortunately, local opposition won the day, which means it will stay unspoiled and remain a living testimony to the history of this beautiful region.

Many paths lead to the woods. We take the one immediately to the right of the Hand and Shears when leaving the pub. You can't miss the waymarker that points to a small lane leading into a large field and then an entrance into the woods.

You can turn left or right on reaching the wood and simply walk around the perimeter, or take one of the many paths through the middle. We usually stick to the perimeter, as we got dreadfully lost once when taking a middle way, ending up on a path leading to Long Hanborough. On that occasion it took us an extra half-hour to get home.

This is one of those walks that can take as long as you wish. We usually amble in an anticlockwise direction for about half an hour and then return the way we came. This wood is particularly beautiful during the spring when bluebells transform the earth into a vibrant carpet of blue. And in the autumn you will discover lots of fat juicy blackberries, mushrooms too. Actually Pinsey Wood acts as a refuge for a number of scarce and striking plants once abundant in this area, such as wood anemone, early purple orchid and meadow saffron. But, please if you discover them, look, admire and then walk away without picking them. These wild flowers are precious and should be preserved.

Whilst dogs are welcome here, walkers are requested to keep them under control so that they don't disturb the wildlife.

The Clanfield Tavern, Clanfield

The first time I visited the Clanfield Tavern (Clanfield, near Bampton) was on a Tuesday following an August Bank Holiday Monday. As usual, I left Auntie Liz and Pythius in my trusty Mini while I went in to ask if dogs were welcome, and enquire about the menu.

'Oh, we don't do meals on a Monday,' said the woman behind the bar. 'But today is Tuesday,' I replied. To which she pointed out that as the day before had been a Bank Holiday, then today was Monday, and they didn't do meals on a Monday. Unable to argue with that logic, dog, Liz and I went on to another pub.

Thankfully, the Clanfield Tavern is now in the very capable hands of Tom Gee and The Real Food Pub Company, who moved in just three weeks before the 2007 floods submerged the entire village in water. The floods were so severe, many customers were stranded for three days, spending their nights bunked up in the bar area until they were able to leave.

The damage caused meant that this lovely 17th-century pub, built in mellow Cotswold stone, had to be completely refurbished. Apart from the spacious new contemporary conservatory extension, with its reclaimed oak floors and large doors that can open up the entire space and let the sunshine in, customers visiting now would never guess that the pub was once submerged under several feet of water.

This remains a pub with original oak beams, flagstone floors and roaring log fires. When the Clanfield Tavern was built in 1610, it was named the Mason's Arms. Besides being used as a public house it was also a meeting place for local clubs and societies in days gone past.

Tom boasts that this pub now serves one of the best Bloody Marys in the Cotswolds, but we go there for

Pythius says

I am not allowed to sit under the table in the conservatory, which is a nice airy building, but I don't mind that, because I am allowed in the bar area by the fire and the fires at this pub are impressive. So is the service. The staff are efficient and friendly and treat me with the respect I have come to expect when visiting pubs with Helen.

Thank goodness the walk takes us along a little stream that offers me a chance to play while Helen and Auntie Liz pick blackberries. I admit that on one walk along this route I found myself staring into the eyes of the biggest black bull I have ever seen. He had a ring in his nose and was standing firm and tall as our eyes met. And yes, of course, I was scared. Who wouldn't be? Fortunately he was in a field on the other side of the stream, which was securely fenced in, so he could only approach so far. Helen said he wouldn't have hurt me. She explained that he was probably just curious, having never seen a border collie splashing about in a stream before. But I wasn't going to take any chances; I was up and out of that stream in a flash.

the wide selection of real ale on tap, which changes weekly. The hundreds of beer mats pinned up on the beams by the bar bear witness to the many guest beers served here these days.

We come for the food too, particularly the salads and vegetables, most of which are grown in the garden at the rear of the pub. Pork and air-dried ham produced at a nearby farm in Kelmscott and local free-range chicken frequently feature on the menu too. In other words, the food served here is about as local as it can get.

The walk

This area is riddled with little streams which run into the Thames that flows under Radcot Bridge just two miles down the Radcot Road (A4095), which goes on to Faringdon. The choice of walks, therefore, is impressive, particularly if you have a water-loving dog like Pythius. Because the hedgerows in this area are thick with blackberries during the autumn, this is a walk we take when I want to stock up with fruit for my homemade wine. I picked enough to make two demijohns of blackberry wine on one occasion. Pythius doesn't get bored while we pick as we walk alongside a little stream that he can splash about in while we collect the blackberries.

The walk begins by taking the Radcot Road beside the Clanfield

Tavern, turning left and walking about half a mile down Main Street (the A4095) alongside the little stream that runs through the village. (You can take the lazy way out and simply drive to the beginning of the walk if you wish, parking your car on the side of the road, near Friar's Court.) Just beyond Friar's Court you will discover a little bridge on the right.

Cross the bridge and enter the first field. Keeping the stream on your right hand side it's then a matter of just ambling along the side of the fields until you come to a point where the path obviously turns to the right. By continuing along this path

you will eventually end up on Hill's Lane. Turn right again and you will find yourself back in Clanfield. Turn left when you reach the main road to return to The Clanfield Tavern. The circular walk will take you less than an hour. Should you leave the car on the side of the road, as we often do, then walk as far as Hill Lane and return the way you came.

The Tunnel House Inn, Coates

Uncle John and I discovered the Tunnel House Inn quite accidentally after leaving the Thames Head Inn. One moment we were driving back along the A433 towards Oxford, having visited the source of the Thames; the next we found ourselves making one of those impulsive left-hand turns one's inclined to do on a fun day out.

Well, there it was – five miles west of Cirencester – a brown sign indicating The Tunnel House Inn and the Sapperton Tunnel. How could we resist? Pythius was delighted when he noted a change of direction, as he knows this could only mean another adventure.

Uncle John was not quite so thrilled when he realised we were approaching an unclassified lane which was both muddy and full of potholes, but he stoically journeyed on – if somewhat cautiously.

After travelling along this lonely unmetalled lane for about a quarter of a mile we reached the Tunnel House Inn, stopped the car and got out to explore. The inn stands proud and firm amidst an undulating landscape which abuts woodland on the Bathurst Estate. Uncle John accepted that we should call in and certainly didn't regret it. Had we just travelled on we would have missed one of the most amazing, zany pubs we have ever encountered.

Built to accommodate the men who were employed to build the 3817-yard-long tunnel, this pub has an austere grey look, but don't let that put you off – it is simply phenomenal.

The first things you notice on entering are the distressed chairs, with their fading tattered fabric offering you a chance to be seated. A pink settee in a similar state dominates the main bar area, which is bedecked with antique advertising signs, old photographs and so much memorabilia you don't know where to look first. A roaring fire with its dancing flames illuminates the artefacts with a glow of red, adding warmth to a pub that was actually warm enough already. It's a chaotic, eclectic mix and that's what makes it so special.

Arriving unexpectedly as we did, with no idea what to expect, we were prepared to be disappointed, yet it turned out to be one of the most remarkable pubs I have ever visited. Pythius appeared to be similarly impressed, particularly when he was offered a bowl of water as soon as he arrived.

Pythius says

Yes, this is a really wacky pub. I loved it. Felt at home straight away. Had a passing dog not sniffed under our table and disturbed me, I would have slept comfortably for as long as was required. Actually I finally felt sorry for him. Apparently this big black Labrador takes himself for a lone walk each day, calling into the pub for company, whereas I have Helen to sort my walks out for me.

I'm always game for a surprise and this walk was certainly that. With all those wet leaves scattered around, I must admit it proved rather slippery at times. I almost fell into the canal at one point because I got so excited. Uncle John and Helen failed to finish this walk once they encountered a tangle of undergrowth and lots of mud, which was a shame; I could have gone on for another couple of miles. I guess we walked about a quarter of a mile or so before turning back. Had we continued we would have eventually met up with the fields we walked when exploring the source from the other end. A jolly romp nevertheless.

And there is more! Having already had lunch, we ordered sandwiches – roast beef and horseradish sauce on granary bread. What we got within minutes was a gourmet's delight! Never have I tasted such a beef sandwich – created from soft luxuriant slices of bread filled with generous slices of succulent warm sirloin beef and oodles of horseradish sauce. After taking the first bite, and declaring our delight at being served such glorious food, Uncle John and I fell into a serious silence as we concentrated on savouring each mouthful. All that remains to be said about this inn is, 'Go and see it for yourselves; you will not be disappointed.'

The walk

Had we continued further when walking to the source of the Thames (see page 99) we would have finally ended up at the village of Coates and the Tunnel House Inn. To walk to the source from this point you can begin by following the drive across the top of the canal tunnel and crossing a stile into the adjoining field, then following a well-worn path. You can also reach the source by walking the canal towpath. We decided to take the latter course by descending the steps besides the tunnel portal. Sadly, despite the valiant attempts of the Cotswold Canals Trust, this disused canal and its towpath are in a state of gentle decay. That said, the portal at the tunnel entrance is a magnificent classical structure, which has obviously been restored with great care. You can only view it properly by taking the steps leading down to the towpath, which Pythius jumped with gay abandon.

Overcome with the beauty of this desolate place, adorned as it was with a kaleidoscope of golden colours created by fallen autumnal leaves, we walked about a quarter of a mile along the track. While Pythius leapt about enjoying an extra walk we absorbed the silence. It was mind-blowing. Nothing (apart from the dog) stirred. For me, this place rates as possibly the most silent in the entire world. The path is slightly overgrown in places, but I understand that had we continued past the Coats Round House, which has also been rescued from further dereliction by the Canal Trust, we would have eventually found the source of the Thames. All we would have had to do was continue under the skew railway bridge for about half a mile to the Trewsbury Bridge. At this point the towpath is no longer a public right of way. You have to turn right onto the bridge and follow the lane down to the field. By following the path (which is well worn and requires no waymarkers) you will come to the source of the Thames, having crossed a couple of fields.

The Radnor Arms, Coleshill

What a great little pub this is. The Radnor Arms stands on the B4019, which runs through the village of Coleshill, and opposite Coleshill Organics. It was once the old smithy for the Coleshill estate, which lies on the western border of Oxfordshire, about five miles from Faringdon.

The estate, which totals some 7,500 acres, consists of 11 farms and 151 cottages, as the villages of Buscot, Coleshill and Eaton Hastings are almost entirely owned by the National Trust. Coleshill Model Farm, known as Courtleaze, stands nearby. It was the home farm of the Earl of Radnor's Coleshill estate. It was built in 1854, a time of relative agricultural prosperity, and made use of the latest agricultural practices and technology, both in building design and livestock management. The majority of the cottages in Coleshill date from the re-modelling of the village during the early mid-19th century by the Earl of Radnor. Only a few homes within the village pre-date the 19th century; these include the pub.

Auntie Liz, Pythius and I visit this area often, as we like buying our fruit and vegetables from Coleshill Organics, and then walking one of the many circular walks around the Coleshill estate, which pass through lush meadows and the most superb countryside.

Obviously we call at the Radnor Arms after the walk. We are always welcome there providing we leave our boots and shoes outside the main door if they are muddy, which is no hardship.

Pythius is allowed in either of the two small bar areas, which you enter through a side door, but not in the restaurant, which is decorated with an abundance of old farming implements that hang from the ceiling and cover the walls. He is served a bowl of water promptly on request, by a team of kindly and very efficient bar staff.

The food here, which is absolutely scrumptious, is sourced locally. The fruits and vegetables come from Coleshill Organics and the meat comes from nearby Kelmscott and other local farms. Occasionally free-range guinea fowl from

Pythius says

We often sit outside when we visit the Radnor Arms, as they have a nice garden behind the car park and a patio area by the side door, which is also the main entrance. The first time we visited this pub was a Monday, and to our dismay we discovered that they don't open on a Monday. So we just did the walk instead. Now we call in the middle of the week, and the staff kindly let me settle my paws under the table near the bar. A bowl of water in a proper stainless steel doggie water bowl is brought promptly by bar staff who always treat me with great respect. Perhaps that's because I am a border collie and this pub caters for a farming community. They know a dog that was reared on a farm and comes from farming stock when they see one. (Did I tell you that I was born on a farm, and that my mother and father used to herd sheep?) Well, I was and they did. I come from an award-winning bloodline of working border collies, and naturally this shows. Farmers can immediately tell I am special, which is why I like visiting areas such as Coleshill. They respect me.

Do I need to comment on a walk, which requires me to stay on a lead for the entire time, and tantalises me with a lovely little stream that I am not allowed to enter? I think not. Yes, the scenery is simply stunning, the meadows lush and the air fresh, but I admit to feeling somewhat restrained when walking the estate. Fortunately Helen and Auntie Liz make this a short walk; I'm not sure how I would cope if I were kept on a lead for four whole miles.

Fairford appears on the menu. Auntie Liz and I usually go for their freshly cut baguettes because the beef or baked ham fillings simply melt in the mouth. I'd rate their baguettes among the best I have ever tasted.

The barrels of real ale, which stand behind the bar, are from small microbreweries, many of which are local. Although food rates high at this pub, it has retained its unspoiled nature, and still attracts local customers who come here for the beer and a chat. In other words, it is still a real country pub in every respect.

The walk

If you call in at the National Trust estate offices, which are signposted to the left once you have passed the Radnor Arms, you can pick up a leaflet detailing five circular walks around the estate. We always park in the estate yard, opposite the line of old red brick pigsties. Having left the yard, we turn left and walk a little way up the hill until

we reach a short lane leading to a farm gate and a series of wonderful fields.

Although visitors are free to walk the footpaths of the estate, they have to respect certain rules: Leave gates and property as you find them. Leave plants where they grow. Take your litter home. Keep dogs on leads to protect wildlife and livestock. Keep to the designated paths.

This means that Pythius doesn't rate the estate as highly as other places he visits as he always feels restricted when kept on a lead. However, the countryside is so beautiful, it's well worth a visit. We take a short walk, which lasts less than an hour. Other walks are about four miles and obviously take a little longer.

Having reached this farm gate you will see a small cottage in the distance on the right hand side. By walking toward the field boundary, you will discover a wooden gate, which leads to a path and the cottage. Keep to this path which winds round towards and past the cottage and keep walking. Eventually you will come to Waterloo Copse on the left. When you come to the end of the copse you will discover a wooden gate and waymarker on the right hand side, which runs alongside a small stream, which joins the River Cole further up. Unfortunately the stream is fenced off, so Pythius cannot paddle or splash about, as he would like to. But he enjoys the walk nevertheless, and walks happily by the stream, admiring the wild watercress, which grows in abundance in its waters.

Half way along this part of the walk you will meet a wooden gate on your left and spot another gate which you reach by walking across the meadow. This is the last gate, and it leads to the original path and back to the village.

The New Inn, Coln St Aldwyns

May I suggest that you visit the New Inn, Coln St Aldwyns, during the autumn when the leaves on the trees are turning from green to glorious golds and reds. You will not be disappointed, particularly if you drive from the A40 and take the turn to Bibury on the B4425, then left to Coln St Aldwyns about four miles on.

The New Inn is easy to spot as this attractive ivy-clad building stands on the main road that runs through the village. An ample car park is available at the rear through an attractive stone archway that once doubled as a pigeon loft.

The first thing that you notice on entering the inn during the day is that nearly everyone is wearing a backpack as this is serious walking country. When you begin exploring you soon realise why – this area is quintessentially English. Whichever way you look, you see gnarled trees, water meadows and lush, undulating pastures through which the River Coln winds its way towards Lechlade. You will be delighted with the many beautiful homes all built from the mellow Cotswold stone which dominates this area too.

The actual age of the New Inn is not known, but it was certainly operational during the reign of Queen Elizabeth I who decreed that

---

Pythius says

I am always impressed when stylish inns such as this welcome me with as much courtesy as they show their other customers. When I visit this pub, I'm greeted and seated as if I am a really important guest, and should I need it, water arrives promptly. Because so many of the lunch customers are walkers, some having arrived from nearby Bibury, they are a really friendly bunch and often include me in the conversation. I like that.

As for the walk, well, this is not exactly what an active dog like me considers an ideal walk, as I am kept on the lead most of the time. Helen did let me off for a while once as we walked down the lane, then she spotted a notice asking riders to dismount. Assuming that this means that horses use this path, I was called to heel again; all a bit of a bore, actually. Then there's the big black Labrador who lives in the house at the bottom of the lane. He often comes out to chat and is a real bossy-boots.

there should be a coaching inn within a day's travel of every major city for the comfort and security of her subjects.

Dogs are welcome in the bar area and a bowl of water is offered the moment they are settled. Although the New Inn boasts that their lunch service is a casual affair, there's nothing casual about the standard of the food, which is first class. Whilst there are many classic dishes listed on the menu, delicious concoctions such as apple and parsnip risotto are also listed for those who enjoy unusual dishes that they may not cook at home. And during the summer it's well worth ordering a glass of Pimms, one of the specialities of the house.

The walk

The six-mile walk that serious ramblers take begins by turning left on leaving the New Inn and heading for the road signposted to Quenington, then over the second bridge and taking the path on the right which follows the river Coln to Bibury.

However, we take a shorter walk around the village, calling into the parish church of St John the Baptist. Our gentle amble begins by turning right outside the New Inn until we get to the crossroads by the Post Office. We then take the left hand turn and then the next left which is signposted to the church. Unfortunately this lovely church has always been closed when we have visited, but we do take time to walk round the churchyard with its lines of weathered head stones, before continuing down the lane. This lane, which gently leads you to the River Coln, is a delight. Wild flowers abound and gaps in the hedgerow allow glimpses of the homes hidden away out of sight of the main road. On reaching the end of the lane you cross a little bridge over the river and meet the road which takes you back to the village. This walk (perhaps it's best described as a stroll) will take about three-quarters of an hour if you stop now and again to admire the views.

The Puesdown Inn, Compton Abdale

The Puesdown Inn stands back from the road on the right hand side of the A40 half way between Burford and Cheltenham, if you are travelling west. It's an attractive Cotswold stone building that takes its name from ancient English, and means windy ridge. This name is apt as it is positioned on land 250 metres above sea level on the ancient Salt Way, which was used to carry salt by packhorse from Droitwich to the Thames at Lechlade and on to London.

As its name is also an anagram for 'snowed up', it's easy to imagine earlier days when stagecoaches rattled down the turnpike road from Cheltenham to Oxford and people really did get snowed up when they arrived at this 13th-century inn.

Last century the Puesdown Inn went through bad times and was desperately in need of refurbishment. But that was last century. Now it's a vibrant, warm and very friendly inn that has already earned two AA rosettes, thanks to the enthusiasm and insight of Maggie and John Armstrong who took it over at the turn of the century and transformed the place beyond recognition.

Their eclectic tastes have brought this lovely old inn to life. Whilst the exposed stone walls and roaring log fires suggest 'olde world' charm and hospitality, the Hollywood memorabilia, posters from *Time Out* magazine and the many souvenirs from John and Maggie's travels in the Middle East suggest this is no ordinary pub. A couple of African masks by the bar say much about this enterprising couple.

John and Maggie have recently added a second restaurant specialising in delicious freshly prepared thin crust pizzas to eat there or take away. We went for one of their traditional dishes, and enjoyed a mouthwatering lunch of mutton pudding, cooked to an original recipe by Mrs Beaton. Pythius was offered water and was so comfortable; he rolled himself up into a ball beside the roaring log fire and didn't wake up until we had finished our coffee.

By the way, the Puesdown is said to have a ghost. It's a highwayman who was shot in the doorway of the pub, but no one has seen him lately. However during a wedding reception a couple of years ago a waitress

---

Pythius says

It was cold outside and warm inside, so once I'd had a drink of water I curled up in front of the fire and slept while Auntie Liz and Helen tucked into one of John's delicious home-cooked meals. I awoke on hearing the tinkle of coffee cups, and then waited anxiously for my walk to begin. As for a pub ghost – I felt nothing – and dogs know about these things.

All was fine when we got out into the open countryside again and I could do doggie things like roll in the mud. Why Helen got in such a tizzy when she saw the way I'd changed my colour from black and white to brown, I just don't know. Surely she knows that when a dog has been spooked, he has to do something to calm himself down?

There was something spooky about this walk, but I am not sure I can say exactly what it was. Whilst I didn't experience anything ghostly while sleeping in the pub, I must admit to feeling really spooked when we walked through the woods. Auntie Liz and Helen assumed I'd picked up the scent of a fox. No, it wasn't that. It's difficult to explain just what I experienced, but it certainly frightened me, which is why I ran round and round in circles for a while.

---

holding a tray of drinks was knocked over by an invisible force just before the guests arrived. Or so the story goes…

The walk

John and Maggie very kindly gave us a map of local footpaths to help us on our way. However, it was so cold and wet the day we visited the Puesdown that we did not complete the five-mile walk that would have taken us to the villages of Hazleton and Turkdean. We took the left turn outside the inn from the car park and walked 40 yards along the side of the A40 to a bridleway, keeping the dry-stone wall on our right. When we reached a triangular-shaped wood on the left, Pythius got really excited and started running round and round in circles, although we never did discover why. Perhaps he smelt a fox?

After leaving the woods you will find that the path rises gently towards the farm buildings of Hazleton. Had the weather been kinder we would have gone on, but instead we headed to the left, and by following the path finally returned to the Puesdown Inn, having walked a circular route of about a mile and a half. It was so wet and muddy that we embarked on this walk with a black and white dog and returned with a chocolate brown dog who appeared to be as cold and wet as we were.

The Lamb Inn, Crawley

The little hamlet of Crawley is one of those unknown gems that people tend to overlook, despite its close proximity to Witney and Burford. Crawley was once linked with Witney's blanket-making history; however, when the duvet became more popular than the blanket, the industry went into decline. Nevertheless, the old mill close to the River Windrush, where blankets were woven, still dominates the landscape. It has now been converted into a series of industrial units and is as busy as ever.

Like several Oxfordshire pubs, the Lamb's name provides evidence of past connections with the wool trade. This is a simply glorious little country pub. Its roaring log fires, flagstone floors, striking inglenoonk fireplace and gnarled beams offer everything one could expect of a pub situated in the middle of nowhere.

Thanks to Matt and Lynne Tucker, who took it over recently, a warm welcome is also assured as this enterprising couple have brought an air of professionalism to an old pub that deserves to be busy.

On entering the bar area you will notice that the name Sebastian hangs over the fireplace. Apparently this pub is haunted. Staff on late duty who are left to lock up at night often hear footsteps shuffling around the bar and upstairs. They believe it must be the footsteps of a licensee long gone, who still wants to be involved with the running of the pub. So they have named him Sebastian and honoured his presence by displaying his name in a prominent place. They are convinced he may stop prowling if he knows he's now an accepted member of the team.

The Lamb is a Brakspear pub which means that fantastic real ales such as Oxford Gold and Brakspear Best Bitter, brewed just a couple of miles away at Wychwood Brewery in Witney, are always on tap.

Food lovers will be delighted to note that the names of the food producers who supply the pub are also displayed prominently for all to see. Matt, who is highly respected for his cooking, prides himself on sourcing his produce locally when possible. We usually go for a bowl of his flavoursome home-made soup, which is a meal in itself, or his home-baked steak pies that come with mouth watering short-crust pastry and local vegetables.

Pythius says

I rather like the fact that the pub ghost is being respected. He's a friendly ghost; that much is certain – border collies can sense such things. My canine instincts tell me they have got his name wrong, though. I am sure he's called Fred, not Sebastian – that name is far too posh. A country pub landlord needs a country name – Fred is far more suitable. Nevertheless, rather the wrong name than no name at all. Since Matt and Lynne took over the Lamb it has become a very happy, bustling place which never fails to welcome me in style. I like it here.

And what a walk! I could ask for nothing more. Loads of water, loads of space and loads of mud. I love it. Added to which there is the mounting excitement as I approach the old ruins that certainly are haunted. Although I haven't met  the doggie ghost yet, I am sure he is there. The ghosts are most apparent when you enter the circular dovecote; I feel goose bumps running up and down my tail when we enter. And my nose goes all twitchy. Once during a cold winter's day I was convinced that something unseen was sniffing my unmentionables. I stood very still and didn't react to this invasion of my privacy – finally the sniffing stopped and I was able to relax.

Pythius likes this pub as the staff respect his need for a bowl of cold water, which is served promptly. Once he is settled, they leave him alone so that he can sleep off the walk. He likes that too.

The walk

This three-and-a-half mile circular walk is so well signposted you just can't go wrong. It hardly needs instructions. Because it offers wooded areas, meadows, a meandering river and streams, as well as the 15th-century ruins of Minster Lovell Hall and the small village of Minster Lovell, it provides virtually everything a walker could wish for. It's easy walking too, though there are some rather muddy areas on the approach to the ruins.

Turn right out of the Lamb and right again along Dry Lane and a bridge that is controlled by traffic lights. Once over the bridge, cross the road and follow the bridleway sign opposite the Old Mill, which will take you away from the road for a while.

When you come to a path junction, put your dog on the lead as you will now turn right through the bridlegate, up the hill and across Dry Lane once more. The path now follows the River Windrush. You will

notice areas fenced off which you are not permitted to walk as this land is managed under the Environmentally Sensitive Area scheme. But as walkers have so much space available to them, this really doesn't matter.

You will pass through meadows and small wooded areas on the approach to the ruins and the church of St Kenelm, which is tucked behind the old hall. When viewed from a distance on an autumnal day with mist drifting through the crumbling ruins, this is an enchanting sight. It's certainly easy to believe this remarkable place is haunted. But not with Sebastian – the Lamb is his territory.

No one is entirely sure who the ghost is. Indeed it is thought that there might be more than one ghost and perhaps the ghost of a little dog too, who died with his master, the first Viscount Lovell. They are thought to have died together, trapped in a basement room, having fled the Battle of Bosworth. The discovery of a man's skeleton sprawled across a table, with the bones of a little dog at his feet, adds weight to this theory. However, the hall is also linked with the legend of the Mistletoe Bow and the young bride who became trapped in a trunk on her wedding day. So all in all there's plenty to ponder on as you walk through these atmospheric stones.

Payment was once required before you could visit the ruins, but no charge is asked now, though you are asked to keep your dog on the lead while walking through both ruins and churchyard, which according to the sign on the gate are open at all reasonable times. I have never quite worked out what would be considered reasonable when visiting a haunted place. Perhaps midnight is out of bounds?

Leaving the ruins you pass through the churchyard, crossing a stone stile which leads to a couple of fields and Minster Lovell's Marsh Meadow and recreation ground. On leaving Marsh Meadow, turn right towards The Old Swan and up the lane to the right through this sleepy little village. Ignore the turning to the church. Beyond Manor Farm look for the footpath on the right which cuts diagonally across a field, leading to a hedgeline path that will take you into Crawley and the Lamb. Views of the Windrush Valley with its dumpy willow trees that follow the river enhance this walk further as you near the end.

The Strickland Arms, Ducklington

The Strickland Arms stands tucked away from the Witney Road that runs through the village of Ducklington near Witney. It's easy to pass this pub without noticing it, which is a shame because it is one of those gems that offers old fashioned hospitality and great food.

Besides which, it is also dog-friendly. The last time that Pythius and I called in we were greeted by the sound of the landlord Andrew Laizen singing away happily to taped music without a care in the world. He was so wrapped up in his music that Pythius finally gave out a gentle bark to announce our arrival.

The best way to describe the interior of the Strickland Arms is to suggest it is just the sort of pub you would like to find in a rural area, such as Ducklington. It is warm and cosy and there's a large fireplace which adds even more character to the main bar when it's lit during the winter.

This is a pub that exudes an air of friendliness. Staff certainly do all they can to make their customers feel welcome and the locals propping up the bar as they enjoy a pint or two of the real ales on tap, also extend a hearty welcome.

The food, which is all home-cooked, is surprisingly good and there is no shortage of seasonal vegetables on the plate. Local meat features on the menu too. On Tuesday evenings, the regular menu changes and customers can have a special offer set meal for a very reasonable price.

The Strickland Arms is just a short walk from St Bartholomew's Church and the 10-acre meadow where one of the most beautiful and rarest of native flowers, the snakeshead fritillary, bursts into bloom each year towards the end of April. Nature lovers from all over the

Pythius says

Nice little pub, this one – it's really friendly. I am made to feel just as welcome as everyone else who comes into the bar. Water is always available and a few pats on the head are usually forthcoming by the kindly customers who sit by the bar. The family that runs this pub seem to like dogs as much as people, which is nice.

I must admit I'm not sure what all the fuss is about with these fritillaries. A flower, is a flower, is a flower! However Auntie Liz and Helen get really excited about Fritillary Sunday, so who am I to argue?

It's all a bit of a bore for a dog while we walk up the main road through Ducklington to the church, and even more of a bore when I discover that I am kept on a tight lead when we reach the duckpond. There are times when Helen is a real spoilsport and all because I got carried away once and forgot that she was on the end of my lead.

Well, I admit she got wet, but not *that* wet. Auntie Liz offered her coat when she discovered Helen was shivering and a spare pair of doggie-walking shoes were soon unearthed from the boot of the car. There was an old beanie hat and a scarf there too. As for her hair, well that didn't take long to dry. The duck I was chasing flew away quite happily; the couple of feathers stuck in my teeth didn't seem to stop it flying away with ease.

When we get to the fritillary field, they both take it in turns to admire the flowers, while I am kept under strict control behind the gate. But that's OK, because once that is all over I get to run the fields that lead to the lake if the sheep aren't out. If they are, then the lead-walk continues until we get to the lake, which is tedious. It's all worth it, however, when we get to the lake and I am free to run, and splash about in the water and just do dog-like things.

country visit Ducklington to see this rare beauty. The villagers even stage an annual Fritillary Sunday, and open the field so that visitors can admire this little flower which is only found in a handful of places throughout the country. You will find the date for this event on the internet; just Google 'Snakeshead Fritillary Ducklington' to find the date the field is open in any particular year.

The walk

Turn right when you leave the pub and walk along the road until you come to the village duckpond and church. This is the point where I put Pythius on a short lead, because if I don't he will try to chase the village ducks that congregate round the pond. The first time Pythius and I took this walk with Auntie Liz, I didn't hold his lead firm enough and ended up in the pond with the ducks. But that's another (and rather soggy) story.

On Fritillary Sunday you will find crowds of people walking past the church and toward the fritillary field, having passed the Ducklington Morris performing their country dances and lots of small stalls selling plants, jam, and home-made cakes for charity.

Walk on down the lane, over a little bridge for about a quarter of a mile and you will reach the fritillary field. Obviously dogs are not encouraged to walk the field, so Auntie Liz and I take it in turns to go in. When you first look at the field, you would be forgiven for wondering just what all the fuss is about, but once you adjust your eyes and really look, you will discover that hundreds of little fritillary flowers are peeping out of the meadow grasses. It's a fascinating sight.

There would be more fritillaries growing in Oxfordshire had it not been for the push for food production during World War II which led to many fritillary fields being ploughed up. This is a flower that only grows in undisturbed meadows. Somehow the Ducklington field escaped this fate and is now sympathetically farmed so that this lovely flower is preserved.

Having paid homage to the fritillary, we usually turn left down a green path that leads to a series of fields and eventually the man-made lake, which we can also reach if we take the walk from The Fleece, Witney (see page 135 for details of this walk).

The Victoria Inn, Eastleach Turville

It would be easy to drive through Eastleach Turville without spotting the pub if it wasn't for a sign placed on the roadside, indicating that it stands just up the bank opposite. Even when you turn to check exactly where the Victoria Inn is, you may have to look twice to confirm it's not just another of the lovely mellow-stoned houses that make up this sleepy little village.

Eastleach Turville may be only four miles from Lechlade, but it seems far off the beaten track, and so unspoiled you will feel you have entered a period film set. No empty plastic bottles litter the streets and there are no Keep Out signs anywhere.

A private house from the 18th century, the Victoria didn't become a pub until 1856. As there are now no shops or businesses in Eastleach Turville, this pub is the focal point of the village. Actually, it's the focal point of two villages, as only the river Leach separates Eastleach Turville from Eastleach Martin. An ancient clapper bridge links the villages and their two parish churches are built but 300 yards from each other. It's all picture postcard stuff. The pub certainly doesn't disappoint, even though the interior is decorated in what is best described as basic pub furniture that probably dates back to the 1970s.

Don't be alarmed if the locals welcome your arrival immediately you enter the pub and invite you to join in their conversation – this is part of the charm. Pythius

Pythius says

When a dog like me is complimented on his glossy coat and shining eyes when he enters a bar – it's about as good as it gets. I love the fact that everyone chats to everyone else in this pub. It's got a sort of homely feel, which is comforting for a border collie. I am usually asked if I would like water when I visit, but I usually refuse as a visit to the Victoria also means a walk along the banks of the River Leach. The water that flows in this river is so fresh and sweet that it's good enough to drink in plenty; it's far superior to tap water, actually. And I should know: I drink enough of it.

This is not one of those walks where I arrive home exhausted having walked miles and miles. It's a walk that I enjoy nevertheless, especially during the spring when hundreds and hundreds of daffodils line the riverbank. (Yes, dogs do appreciate flowers!)

Auntie Liz and Helen usually sit by the little stone bridge and let me potter about in the water – I love that as it's not muddy and, as I said, the water is crystal clear and tastes as sweet and pure as any water I have ever tasted.

I guess you would describe this as a pottering sort of walk, with time set aside to watch the swans if they appear. I'm immediately pulled out of the water if they do appear, as dogs and swans with their cygnets simply don't mix. Well – that's what Helen says, and I have to accept that she does get it right now and again. So I'm yanked out to join them on the bridge where we all sit and watch as the swan family swims past. Actually it's really lovely – so peaceful.

adores the fact that locals put down their pints of Arkells real ale when he arrives, and having asked his name begin talking about the many border collies they have known and owned over the years.

There's a spacious restaurant area, but when Pythius is with us, we are invited to eat in the bar, or take a table outside and enjoy a view that probably hasn't changed for centuries. We usually remain in the bar, as Pythius is always much taken by the local residents who continue to chatter to him throughout our stay.

Food doesn't arrive in a hurry even though the well-balanced menu is not large. This is because every meal is cooked to order, including delicious hand-cut chips, which taste as good as the ones that mother used to make. Seasonal local produce and British food features large on the menu, which usually includes Eastleach Downs organic pork sausages and pork chops.

The walk

This area is festooned with footpath markers, many of which are carved in wood and appear to have been erected many years ago. You can cross the clapper bridge and take the footpath to Fyfield or Southrop if you want a long walk, or you can pick up the Roman road, Akeman Street, which linked St Albans to the Fosse Way. But if you want to simply soak up the silence that envelopes this lovely area, visit the two villages and watch the swans and their

cygnets gliding down the river; you can take a circular walk round Eastleach Martin and Eastleach Turville. The timeless atmosphere of these villages is so phenomenal, a short walk is not to be scoffed at when taken at a leisurely pace. By turning left after leaving the pub and taking the lower road, you will soon arrive at the river. Cross the clapper bridge, constructed from large slabs of stone supported on stone piles, and you will reach the other bank with its footpath leading to the church of St Michael and St Martin. This church incorporates the original 12th-century nave and a Norman south doorway. John Keble was once the curate here. As he went on to become a founding member of the Oxford Movement, author of many hymns and a major influence on the Church of England, the clapper bridge was named after him. A fund in his memory founded Keble College, Oxford, which still owns considerable amounts of land in this area.

From this church, you can return the way you came and visit the church of St Andrew, at the north of the village and admire its Norman saddle-back tower before returning to the river to watch the swans.

The Queen's Head, Queen Street, Eynsham

This is Pythius' local. It's here that he gets to meet several of his canine friends. Besides, a visit here is inevitably followed by a walk through the playing fields and the newly restored fishponds that date back to the time when Eynsham boasted a very grand abbey.

The Queen's Head is one of six pubs in the village (seven if you count the Evenlode Beefeater on the A40). Although this pub first opened in 1850, there's been some kind of ale house on this site since 1600.

The Queen after whom the pub was named was Queen Anne, who reigned from 1702 to 1714. She was the monarch who gave Blenheim to the Duke of Marlborough. You will find the original picture used to create the pub sign in the old bar. You will also find a superb collection of railway memorabilia on display here that dates back to the days when Eynsham had its own railway station.

This popular pub, the haunt of the local cricket team and many of the talented artists that reside in Eynsham, is known for good conversation and an excellent choice of real ales.

Pythius says

This is the pub where I can meet up with all my four-legged friends. They too appreciate the bowl of cool water placed close to the bar to keep us happy while our owners enjoy a bacon buttie and a glass of Timothy Taylor's Landlord or one of the many other real ales on tap here.

Sometimes we all congregate outside in the garden in the summer, as there are bowls of water there too.

I hate the fact that Helen keeps me on a lead while we walk though the playing field, but that's what she has to do. All dogs must be kept on a lead – that's the rule. The walk only improves once we enter the fishponds area where I can run free and enjoy the smells of rabbit and the occasional deer, providing I keep reasonably close to Helen and do not disturb ground-nesting birds. I can also paddle and enjoy rolling in the muddy edges of the main pond when Helen is not looking. This walk is not long, no more than half a mile, but it's perfect when taken at the end of the day.

It's one of those rare pubs that have not succumbed to a modern makeover. Although inside toilets and a commercial kitchen were added in 1993, the public bar has remained untouched for more than 150 years, which is another reason why the villagers love it so much. Pythius loves it too.

Although you can enjoy a delicious doorstep-sized bacon buttie and chips at lunch time, it's the wide choice of real ales always available for which this pub is known. Thanks to Pete the friendly licensee's excellent beer-keeping skills and the cool, dark cellar built directly under the bar that helps stabilise the beer at the right temperature, a pint drunk here is one to remember.

The walk

By turning right as you leave the Queen's Head and then left when you get to the main road that runs through the village, you will reach the village playing fields on the right-hand side in a matter of minutes. It's here that you will find two cairns built from stones that were originally collected by villagers when Henry VIII closed the abbey in 1538. These cairns provide a history of the area and a map that guides the walker through the main field to the fishponds area on the right. This land was originally purchased by Abbot Adam in the early 13th century to increase the abbey's prosperity and provide the monks with ponds that would keep them supplied with fresh fish. Following the destruction of the abbey, this seven-acre site remained relatively untouched for 400 years. It was recently restored to its original glory by hard working volunteers who worked tirelessly to reinstate the ponds and tame the tangled undergrowth. Now the area acts as feeding ground to more than 33 species of birds, including kingfishers and cuckoos, and provides villagers and visitors with a peaceful area in which to walk. Having passed through the fishponds by following the trail you will come out at Station Road, which is close to where Auntie Liz lives, but you want to return to the Queen's Head, so simply keep to the path on the right when you approach this road and you can do a full circle, ending up back at the playing fields.

The Talbot
Oxford Road, Eynsham

Yes, another Eynsham pub, but this one is quite different from my local, the Queen's Head. The Talbot is our summer pub, as it lies a few hundred yards beyond the village boundaries and we only go there in fine weather. The Talbot stands back from the Oxford Road besides a pretty little stream and it's but a stone's throw from the Swinford toll bridge that spans the Thames.

This bridge, built in 1769, is one of the finest bridges over the Thames, constructed during the golden age of Georgian architecture when both design and craftsmanship were very good. That said, Eynsham residents who use it daily to get to Oxford via Botley, constantly complain about the long delays when crossing the bridge during peak hours. They also find it a bother when they discover they have no loose change in the glove box and have to fumble in their pockets on their approach to the bridge for the 5p toll.

The Talbot is an Arkell's pub which serves a good pint. I usually go for their Summer Ale, which is an excellent light beer that's just what you crave on a balmy summer evening whilst sitting outside on the

decking abutting the little stream that runs besides the pub.

During the summer months, The Talbot serves food throughout the day. The menu is standard pub fare and obviously includes fish and chips which is always nicely served and reasonably priced. Thanks to recent renovations the dining area has been revamped, but not too much. It still has a great deal of character; in fact it has probably got more character now than it had before. The bar area with its limestone finish has remained untouched, which is fine by the locals, particularly the allotment holders who call in for a pint at the end of the day, having worked hard on their plots nearby.

This pub attracts walkers too, as the footpath besides the stream leads to some superb river walks. Dogs are allowed inside in the bar area providing they are kept under control.

The walk

There's a footpath beside the pub that follows the little stream, passing a couple of factories on the left-hand side along the way. Once past the factories, you approach a kissing gate that leads to a series of meadows and the River Thames. We tend to follow the stream,

> ### Pythius says
>
> We usually visit the Talbot in the early evening. I get to enjoy my walk first then we call in for a quick drink before going home. I am allowed inside, but only if I sit quietly and don't argue with any other dogs using this pub. However, I like it best when we sit on the decking outside, as I love watching the swans swimming along the stream while I relax after a long walk. My only gripe is that this pub is right next to the Oxford Road, which gets very busy at times. I hate traffic fumes! I hate the noise of traffic too! It spoils the feeling of peace and tranquillity that dogs like me appreciate so much.
>
> I admit to blotting my copybook the day we first walked towards the Thames. Well, how was I to know that Helen would make such a fuss when I cooled myself off by rolling in a couple of moist cow pats in the cow field? It smelt so good at the time and was wonderfully squashy. Gosh she was mad. Ordered me straight back to the stream and insisted I stayed there until I had removed all that lovely smelly brown stuff. It was some while before we did the cow field walk again. Now I know the rules and remain in the first meadow, stopping my run through the grasses occasionally to paddle about in the little stream, then Helen tends to relax. We take this walk often now. Actually, it's one of my favourites.

keeping it to our right, crossing a couple of stiles before arriving at a little wooden bridge spanning the stream. This leads to a large field where cows graze in the summer.

Pythius tends to stop when we approach this bridge and will happily splash about in the stream for hours if we let him. We seldom venture in the field if the cows are grazing, though by crossing this field we can get to Eynsham lock, where a small footbridge will take us to the other side of the river and the Thames Path: turn left here and you can follow the boundaries of Wytham Woods, and get to Godstow and the Trout in about 3 miles. Turn right and pass Pink Hill lock and follow the riverside path to Bablock Hythe and beyond. Because there are so many choices, this is a great place to take the dog providing you remember that they are banned from Wytham Woods. Indeed human members of the public are banned from these ancient woods too, unless they have obtained a walker's permit from Oxford University who use the woods to research zoology and climate change.

The Five Alls, Filkins

Filkins is one of those little Cotswold villages that are easy to pass by when travelling along the A361 from Burford to Lechlade. People notice the Cotswold Wildlife Park on the right, but too often fail to appreciate that a left turn to Filkins just a couple of miles on down the road will take them to a quintessential Cotswold village, with its own community shop and a glorious pub.

This is the village that won the Calor Village of the Year Award in the Building Community Life category in 2006/7 and where you will find the Cotswold Woollen Weavers Wool Heritage Centre. The village pub is an 18th-century coaching inn, the Five Alls, which can be found on the road that winds through the village.

People are always puzzled by its name. What does it mean? Is there a spelling mistake? Did the sign-writer mean to write Five Ales? No – not so. If you look at the sign you will see that the head of the devil is painted in the centre, surrounded by a lawyer who pleads for all, a parson who prays for all, a soldier who fights for all and a farmer who pays for all. In other words all your needs are sorted, but the devil governs all.

The Five Alls is a really lovely pub. Its three interconnecting rooms, with exposed Cotswold stone walls, flagstone floors and chunky wooden ceiling, are charming. This is one of those pubs which manages to retain a happy friendly atmosphere even when there are only a few people inside. A delightful little black spaniel acts as 'meeter and greeter' when you open the door. He will even escort you to the bar if you wish. Pythius was not sure that he liked being shown where to sit by another dog, but we sorted that in the end. Pythius ducked under the nearest table, and the spaniel dashed to the door to say hello to the next customer.

It's a Brakspear pub, serving beers that have been brewed a few miles away at Wychwood Brewery, Witney. This means that real ale lovers are able to indulge themselves and enjoy brews such as Oxford Gold or Hobgoblin.

The menu reflects both the seasons and the local food scene. Very local pork and beef are roasted daily during the summer months and freshly harvested vegetables are served according to season. Because

Pythius says

I know that the house dog was only trying to be hospitable, but being escorted to our table by a spaniel – well, it was a bit humiliating. It's bad enough having Helen telling me what to do and where to go all the time, but to be ordered about by a dog – I can definitely do without it. Helen called him a sweet little fellow, kept patting his head and stroking him under the chin. That didn't go down well with me either. However, this is a nice pub. There's a great big bowl marked DOG in the main bar and one outside the main door.

As walks go, this wasn't bad at all. There was lots of lovely squishy mud along the little path through the coppice, which I enjoyed a great deal, although it caused Auntie Liz and Helen a few problems. Then came the big open field where I could run and run and run. Oh what fun I had. The best of all was the stream, of course, even though it was bulging with watercress plants, which caused me a few problems when the ball I was chasing vanished under a great big clump. I got a bit tangled up at that point but soon sorted it out. Helen and Auntie Liz stayed on the little stone bridge while I splashed about to my heart's content once I was free to move again.

Helen is right about the stone stile at the end of the walk. It is tall, very tall. I could have jumped it, but might have been in trouble as I landed the other side as there's a big railway sleeper in place to help people get over. I had to stay outside while Helen and Auntie Liz took it in turns to walk round the Cotswold Wool Heritage Centre. Helen came out carrying a lovely new winter scarf and Auntie Liz bought a warm pair of gloves. Nothing for me, of course; not even some ear warmers, but that's how it goes sometimes.

this pub serves home-made chips and makes their batter with Brakspear ale, Auntie Liz and I usually go for the fish and chips, which taste scrumptious – lovely light batter, moist fish and crunchy chips just like mother used to make.

The walk

I had packed a map in my rucksack so that we could find a suitable walk when we got to Filkins, but I needn't have bothered. The landlord's local knowledge of dog walks proved second to none. First he asked us how many miles we wanted to walk; then asked what we wanted from the walk. After a moment's thought he came up with a lovely half-mile stroll that incorporated a few large fields where Pythius could run and a little stream where he could splash about afterwards.

The walk begins by turning left out of the pub and walking along the road, past a magnificent yew hedge on the left, then St Peter's Church and then the war memorial until you get to Rouses Lane, also on the left hand side. A red letterbox marks the spot.

Walk down the lane, past the village shop with its blue plaque dedicated to Sir Stafford Cripps, statesman and bene-

factor to the village, until you come to a stile which leads to a rather muddy path through a coppice. Guernsey cows in the field to the left may walk over and vie for your attention; they are very beautiful. You eventually leave this path and enter a large grassy field. It's easy to see where you have to go immediately as this is a well-worn path marked out by countless footsteps. The path turns into another field and a watercress stream and then on to the rear of the Cotswold Wool Heritage Centre.

There is an exceptionally tall stone stile that leads to a lane and the main street back through the village. We chose to let ourselves into the Cotswold Wool Heritage Centre's car park though a gate instead, as even Pythius was concerned about the height of this stile. Unfortunately dogs are not allowed into the centre; otherwise we could have stopped there for a cup of tea.

The Plough Inn, Finstock

How we enjoy the approach to the Plough as we drive down Finstock High Street, having taken a turning off the B4022 which runs from Charlbury to Witney. The view, as you travel down the hill and head towards The Bottom, is superb, particularly when the neat thatched roof of the Plough comes into view. Yes, that's its address – The Bottom – because this delightful Grade II listed building stands at the bottom of the hill, set amid rolling Cotswold countryside.

The name Finstock is said to mean 'the place frequented by woodpeckers', although we have never spotted one during our many walks in this area. Perhaps that's because they reside in Wychwood Forest, where an abundance of ancient trees on which woodpeckers rely for both food and nesting sites are found in plenty. At one time, many of the villages round here were clearings in the forest; now the much-diminished forest lies mostly to the west of Finstock.

Like so many pubs, the Plough began life as a small house probably built for a farm labourer. If the date 1772 which is inscribed in the keystone of the lintel over the entrance is correct, it became an alehouse within five years of being built.

Naturally all those features you would expect from an old country pub are in place, including a large inglenook fireplace where roaring log fires are kept topped up throughout the winter months.

The Plough rates as one of Pythius' favourite pubs, due in part to the fact that he is sometimes given a pig's ear to chew when he returns home. He is very partial to pigs' ears, and the proprietors Joe and Martin know this.

As this is a free house, the choice of real ales and draught ciders has earned the pub a place in CAMRA's *Good Beer Guide*. No doubt they will soon be earning similar accolades for the quality of their food. Even a plate of fish and chips is a gourmet's delight, though it is the produce that Joe and Martin acquire locally which features large on this menu. Their aim is to serve as much locally sourced food as possible in a glorious 'pubby' atmosphere. Sitting besides the fire, tucking into a large plate of Joe's home-cooked beef stew and herbed dumplings, is my idea of heaven, especially after a long walk on a chilly day. This is British

Pythius says

Helen's right – The Plough is certainly one of my favourite pubs. Joe and Martin are so sensitive to my needs. After a long walk during the winter months I am assured of a warm fire, a bowl of water and a real welcome. The pig's ears? Well, they are just a little extra that comes my way from time to time. What dog could ask for more?

What Helen has not mentioned are the pheasants! During the autumn and winter months this walk is absolutely loaded with pheasants! They jump out in front of me with no warning at times. Naturally I would give chase if Helen didn't call me back in that stern voice of hers. Sometimes they are running in front of me, waddling awkwardly as they make their dash for freedom. I tasted pheasant stew once, so I know how delicious they can be, but I've never tasted one in the raw – unfortunately! Then there are the horses. Helen is right; you never know when you are going to come face to face with a horse and rider in this area, so I am kept under close control when we walk the narrow (and often very muddy) paths. This means it's not the best of walks for me, but I do love the smells and the atmosphere, as this is unspoiled countryside at its best – but sadly we have never seen or heard a woodpecker, though we have heard their rapid tap, tap, tap as they break through the bark of a dead tree to find their dinner.

food at its best. And for those just seeking a snack at lunchtime, there's an excellent range of light snacks and sandwiches too.

It's thanks to Joe and Martin that this book came into being. Until speaking to them, *Paws Under the Table* was just a pipe dream. Because they knew Pythius and my love of good food, they encouraged me to take it further.

The walk

Footpaths have traversed the Finstock area for generations. Akeman Street runs a few hundred yards behind the pub and a lot of Roman coins are found round here. More recent paths such as the Wychwood Way also connect with a network of footpaths and bridleways in the Finstock area.

Pythius rather enjoys a ramble down Dark Lane, which is found opposite the Plough, though we sometimes take the footpath at the rear

of the pub which comes out on Blackbird Assarts Lane, if you keep going straight, straight, straight. However, you can take a right hand turn at the top of the field and circle back to the pub if you wish.

Dark Lane actually lives up to its name in places, as there are moments when the trees and vegetation either side of the path do seem to weigh in on you. But if you keep going, you will come to a waymarker a hundred yards before you get to the River Evenlode and the railway line. It points to the right, taking you up a track called Topples Lane and then through Topples Wood (so called because it covers the site of the deserted village of Tapwell). This walk, which takes half an hour or more, can prove very muddy at times, but we like it as it's very atmospheric. You feel the weight of centuries pressing down on you as you go. Eventually, having passed through Topples Wood, you will arrive at a small road, where dogs have to be put on a lead, as it gets very busy at times. Turn right and you will be back at the Plough within 10 minutes.

Or extend the walk by turning left and following the lanes into the hamlet of Wilcote, where a footpath almost opposite the Norman church will return you across the fields to Finstock in half an hour or so.

One word of warning: this is a horsy area and you may encounter a rider and horse during this walk, so don't let your dog run round blind corners or get too far ahead of you.

The Lamb Inn,
Great Rissington

Great Rissington is one of those picturesque little Cotswold villages capable of taking your breath away because it is so unspoiled and beautiful. It stands just three miles south-east of Bourton-on-the-Water.

The Lamb Inn was originally a farmhouse, the oldest parts of which date back 300 years. Had the Wellington bomber flying over Great Rissington one black night in 1943 crashed just ten yards further on, this superb Cotswold inn would not be standing now. The bomber was making for the nearby RAF Little Rissington airfield, but ended up in the garden of the Lamb instead. Just one member of the crew survived, which is why his letters and aircraft memorabilia are displayed in the main bar.

The Lamb stands in the centre of the village and overlooks the Windrush valley. You enter the bar area down a series of steps, which I fear people with hip problems may find rather difficult. I certainly did when Pythius became over exuberant and rather excited about being taken out to lunch, almost pulling me down the steps in his dash to get inside.

Despite rushing into the bar, however, he was welcomed in style as this is a very dog-friendly pub. It welcomes walkers too. The day we arrived the bar was already filled with a party of ramblers tucking into the reasonably priced soup-and-sandwich option. The perfect lunch after a long walk on a chilly day.

The Lamb does have a stylish restaurant, but at lunchtime most visitors appear to use the bar areas, one of which is full of second-hand books offered for sale to raise funds for the Guide Dogs For The Blind Association.

The décor with its sports trophies, memorabilia and photographs, is best described as homely and comfortable. You feel this place embracing you the moment you open the door. The customers seem at ease with each other too.

As it's a free house a good selection of local brews are on tap, including several beers from the Hook Norton Brewery.

Pythius says

Helen did get rather mad with me when I pushed past her as she descended the steps into the main bar area. How was I to know she was finding them rather difficult? After all Auntie Liz had managed them perfectly. I just wanted to get my paws under a table so that lunch could begin. The sooner lunch is ordered and enjoyed, the sooner we can get cracking on the walk.

Because the other customers were so friendly, my haste to get lunch over and done with was pointless. Helen and Auntie Liz spent ages lingering over their coffee talking to the other walkers gathered there. As they included me in the conversation, I didn't complain too much.

This is great dog walk. So many delicious smells. Everything is unspoiled and very, very beautiful. Helen does keep me close to her because of the wild life and sometimes puts me on a lead, but not for long. Once we get to the river I am allowed to splash about and have fun, which for me is what it is all about when walking the Cotswolds.

Apparently local ingredients are used at The Lamb Inn whenever possible, Cotswold slow roast lamb being a particular favourite.

The walk

On the advice of the walkers in the bar we turned right on leaving the pub and headed for the church, which lies down the slope of the village street and beside the manor house. As some parts of St John the Baptist church date back to the 12th century, it's well worth a visit, particularly as it boasts carved Norman coffin lids which are set in the grass outside the south transept.

On leaving the church you come to a waymark pointing to a lane that leads to a gate and a stile and then on through a conifer plantation. Bear left when you leave the plantation and follow the next waymark which points diagonally over the field ahead. The next waymark stands close to a small triangular wood on the right. This takes you in the same direction and over another field and a field boundary some 250 yards from the right hand corner of the field. Once you have passed several superb oak trees on the left you are approaching the River Windrush and one of the most beautiful stretches of water in the Cotswolds. We stopped at this point having walked about half a mile and let Pythius have some fun splashing about in the river, then ambled back the way we had come.

Had we wished for a four-mile circular walk we could have kept the river on our right and followed the waymarkers which eventually lead you back to Great Rissington.

It's worth pointing out that this area is rich with wildlife, including deer, pheasants, Canada geese and wild duck, so dogs must be carefully controlled at all times.

The Falkland Arms, Great Tew

The rolling hills and countryside surrounding the Falkland Arms are simply amazing, particularly if you visit during the autumn months when the trees are turning from green to gold. There's no doubt that trees are Great Tew's crowning glory and one of the many reasons why this beautiful village with its thatched ironstone cottages was designated an Outstanding Conservation Area in 1978.

Loudon, the 19th-century landscaper, planted most of the trees, particularly the exotic ones in the parkland. He laid out new field patterns at Great Tew too.

Great Tew is five-and-a-half miles east of Chipping Norton and the Falkland Arms stands in the centre of the village, next to the village shop and just a couple of minutes' walk from a small public car park built recently to relieve congestion during the tourist season.

The Falkland Arms, originally named the Horse and Groom, is one of the finest inns in Oxfordshire. It's now named after Lord Falkland who inherited the manor of Great Tew in 1629 and spent the years before the outbreak of the civil war keeping open house to notable poets, philosophers and theologians of the age.

There has been an inn on this site for at least 500 years which becomes apparent when you step inside to be confronted with its remarkable assortment of clay pipes, antique jugs and beer mugs hanging from the heavy gnarled beams in the ceiling. A cosy inglenook fireplace and comforting log fire in the winter, oak panelling, flagstone flooring and high-backed settles confirm this is indeed a very special pub.

Obviously it attracts hundreds of tourists during the summer, which is why Auntie Liz and I only take Pythius there during the autumn and winter months. Not only do we get the bar to ourselves in the winter, but we are able to stride out and enjoy one of the many walks in this area without bumping into too many other walkers.

The food is good; however, the Falkland Arms doesn't pretend to be a gastro pub even though everything is cooked from scratch from local ingredients. I have had some really delicious meals here over the years.

Real ale enthusiasts will be delighted to discover that eight real ale pumps dispense an extensive range of beers, which include four guest beers that are changed regularly to keep discerning drinkers happy. English country wines, such as elderberry and blackberry, and real cider are also available. And if you fancy a pinch of snuff, that's on sale too.

Pythius always walks in as if he owns the place, chooses a place to

Pythius says

We visited this pub during the summer once and it was so crowded we had to sit outside in the garden, which was not the best thing to do as it was as busy outside as it was inside. However, in the winter this pub offers everything I need: a friendly atmosphere, a warm fire and a nice clean floor to curl up on while Helen and Auntie Liz enjoy their lunch.

Yes – I like this walk providing Helen doesn't put me back on the lead too often. I love running and leaping through the stubble which makes a great crackling noise as I go.

Helen and Auntie Liz often just stand and stare when we walk this way, listening to the silence as this lovely place really is quiet. Only the occasional cry from a pheasant disturbs the peace. There's one field filled with sheep on the left, just a couple of fields up the path, which is surrounded by a rather nasty wire fence that gives me a sharp shock if I try to run through it. Not good for dogs or sheep. Otherwise, this is a very nice winter walk with great views.

curl up on the flagstone floor close to the fire, then sleeps contentedly until we have finished our meal and it's time to walk.

The walk

There are loads of walks you can enjoy from here. Auntie Liz and I take the easy option, but should you wish to take a four-mile walk which takes you to Little Tew, then start from the car park, turn left, past the turning to Great Tew, following the road as it bends, then right at the footpath sign to Little Tew, which calls for a diagonal walk across a field to farm outbuildings on the brow of the hill. You will find a stile; climb this, then follow the field boundary until you come to galvanised gates and a stile leading to a road junction. Cross the road and take the path to Little Tew and soon this lovely little village will come into view. By following waymarkers you can then aim for Tracey Barn Farm, and return to Great Tew via St. Michael's Church.

Our easy option requires us to turn left down a small bridle path next to the pub, and then go straight, straight, straight for half a mile or so. On your right you will have Great Tew Park, with its fine trees, where sheep are usually grazing happily; on your left are fields of wheat, rape or sunflowers. If you walk this way in the autumn, however, when the crops have been harvested, you will pass large fields of stubble, which offer your dog space to roam.

The views are breathtaking. It's worth walking this way just to absorb the beauty of this unspoiled area. Once you get to the top of a hill you will find you can turn left, right or go straight on. We turn and leisurely amble back, but you don't have to, at this point the choice is yours.

Because pheasants are reared in this area, you are advised to keep your dog under close control in places. Quite rightly the gamekeepers get very upset if dogs disturb their birds or the wildlife.

The Plough, Kelmscott

Some of my friends consider the South Cotswolds village of Kelmscott to be in the middle of nowhere, although it is just three miles from Lechlade, if you take the A417 and follow the signs. Perhaps they are right – maybe that's why Pythius and I like it so much. Kelmscott is one of those magic places that we visit in the winter, when the tourists have gone and only the plaintive cry of the rooks who nest in the trees beside the Thames disturb the peace.

If you call in during the summer, you will find Kelmscott simply overrun with tourists all hoping to capture something of William Morris's spirit by visiting Kelmscott Manor which Morris, the 19th-century poet, artist and craftsman, made his summer home. Thanks to the cooperation of local planners, the National Trust and the Society of Antiquaries of London, who now own Kelmscott Manor, the peaceful calm of this beautiful little village is assured.

Pythius and I go there for the silence, which is guaranteed when you take a companionable river walk along the Thames during the depths of winter, when it is a desolate and solitary place. We love it for its isolation, even when excessive rainfall creates muddy puddles and the occasional flood.

The Plough is no stranger to floods. Unfortunately it suffered dreadfully during the floods of 2007, and on my last visit to this glorious little village (just days before this book was due to be completed), I was distressed to discover the flood damage has still not been repaired. The doors were closed and barred and the housedog who usually trots down the path to greet us was nowhere to be seen.

I accept that it's inevitable some of the pubs Pythius and I have come to enjoy over the years will change hands or close, but I never thought that I'd have to cross the Plough off my list.

On speaking to several Kelmscott residents during that visit, I was

---

Pythius says

This is a walk Helen and I do on our own now and again. I think she rather enjoys the silence of Kelmscott and the unspoiled wildness of the river walk. It gives her space to think.

Even I can appreciate the beauty of this place. It is unspoiled, natural and very, very lovely. No wonder that famous man Mr Morris loved it so. I often wonder if he had a dog like me when he walked this way. I'd like to think he had. Apparently this countryside inspired him when he was designing his

patterns and furnishings (well, that's what Helen says, and if she says it, it must be true – perhaps?). There's no ball throwing on this walk. We just amble gently along the river bank, watching the swans and coots and listening to the rooks squabbling in their numerous rookeries along the way. Unfortunately, the banks of the river are too deep for me to splash about in the water, but that's OK. There are times when I can cope with that, particularly when I have Helen's undivided attention.

assured there is every chance that the Plough will open again, and soon, which is why it remains listed among our favourite pubs. Besides, Kelmscott village can be used as a starting point to two other Thames-side pubs, if you are prepared to walk about three miles in either direction.

By turning right along the river and heading for Lechlade you will reach the Trout, at St John's Bridge, a glorious little pub that has been offering hospitality to visitors for more than 700 years. Dogs are welcome inside providing they remain in the section of the bar with the flagstone flooring. It's here that you can order a Sunday roast that will probably overwhelm you – the portions are so generous they would be difficult to finish if you hadn't walked three miles to get there. Appetising bar snacks are available too for those who simply can't face a gigantic meal. This is a lovely laid-back pub, with low gnarled beams and roaring log fires in the winter.

Despite the crowds who congregate here during the spring and summer months, the staff cope brilliantly and everyone gets served providing they don't mind forming a queue to obtain a drink and order their food which can be enjoyed inside or in the large pub garden. A water bowl for dogs stands outside the entrance.

If you prefer to take the Thames path left along the river on leaving Kelmscott, you will eventually arrive at the Swan Inn at Radcot Bridge on the A4095, one of three stone bridges between Radcot and Faringdon. Unfortunately dogs are not allowed inside, but are welcome to sit outside in the pub's extensive riverside garden providing they are kept under control. Whilst the food here tends to be basic pub grub, it is nicely served and very tasty.

The walk

The walk we used to take when visiting the Plough is just a mile and a half long, but that's fine by us. Having tucked the car away on one of the side streets we turn sharp left on passing the pub, then take the track at the side of the pub to meet up with a hedged footpath and a footpath heading south. You then come to a double footbridge over a stream that leads to the Thames.

By taking the Thames Path in a north-easterly direction you have at least three quarters of a mile of pleasant walking besides the river, before arriving at a hand-gate which leads back to the village if you bear left. You will eventually arrive on the road outside the gateway to

Kelmscott Manor. Continue along this road, past the Memorial Gardens erected in 1902 by Jane Morris as a memorial to her husband, and you will reach the Plough. But if the Plough is still closed when you visit and you aim to enjoy a pub lunch you will have to remain on the Thames Path and walk a little further.

As Kelmscott stands midway between Radcot and Lechlade you are faced with an enjoyable walk regardless of which direction you take as this is a very pleasant section of the Thames which meanders gently through some beautiful, unspoiled countryside.

By following the Thames Path towards Lechlade you will pass through Buscot lock, which gives you a chance to visit Buscot Manor and Buscot Church, which contains a stunning set of Burne Jones stained glass windows. After passing Buscot you will spot Lechlade's church tower on the horizon and eventually come to an attractive wooden footbridge which links with a footpath that will take you to the other side of the river and on to Lechlade. You reach the Trout however by ignoring the bridge and walking through a small gated lane close to the bridge.

This lane leads to a small road that will take you to the A417: turn left towards the Trout.

If you wish to visit the Swan, turn left on reaching the Thames at Kelmscott and follow the river's gentle twists and turns for about three miles.

The Thames Head Inn, near Kemble

The official source of the River Thames is strongly contested. Some insist that this mighty river begins at Trewsbury while others say the true source can be found at Seven Springs some 11 miles further north. My vote goes for a spot that lies but half a mile from the Thames Head Inn, situated on the A433 between the Gloucestershire towns of Tetbury and Cirencester.

Having visited this spot with my previous border collie Apollo, many years ago, I decided that Pythius ought to visit it too. The Thames Head is a really friendly place. They don't mind you leaving your car in their car park while you visit the source, providing you stop in for a drink on your return.

You will spot a notice by the main entrance asking walkers to remove their muddy boots before entering the bar, which is understandable. Dogs simply have to wipe their paws on the mat! Yes, dogs are welcome here. It's a very dog- friendly pub as three dogs live here: Troy, Buster and Dave, who only enter the bar once the lunch service is over and the bar is empty, which means visiting dogs can make themselves at home.

Pythius was thrilled to discover that he was made really welcome and was free to snuggle up and sleep off his walk on a lovely warm carpet. (Whilst he accepts flagstone floors are attractive, he finds them rather cold at times – carpets offer him the warmth and comfort he needs on a cold day.)

The food served here is great. It rests midway between pub grub and gastro pub grub. Everything is home-cooked and tasty. You certainly won't be disappointed if you go for a big bowl of home-made soup, or a steak and kidney pie cooked in real ale. A specials board which details both restaurant and snack meals adds a few exciting house specialities.

Bunches of wild hops decorate the bar area, which is where your canine companions are welcome and a friendly smile from the bar staff confirms they are pleased to see you, because it's that kind of place.

As it's an Arkells pub you will be able to enjoy a pint of Moonlight

Pythius says

We had to drive quite a long way to get here, but it was worth it, though Helen and Uncle John did keep me waiting a long time as they took off their muddy boots before entering the bar. However, the carpets were so nice, I can understand why the owners don't want them covered with mud.

I found this a very friendly pub, I was offered everything I wanted and no one asked me to wipe my feet, so I tucked them well under the table so that the barman wouldn't notice they were slightly muddy.

Because Helen was scared about crossing the railway line, I was scared too. Dogs like me pick up such vibes. However Uncle John was with us, and he is a very sensible chap. He looked left and then right and then left again and on hearing nothing, ordered us to walk briskly across. Must admit I was glad when that ordeal was over. The few trains that rattle along this track go at a goodly pace.

There were no cows in the field in which the source is marked when we visited during the autumn, however there were positive signs they had been there. There were also loads of signs that Mr Fox visits this area often. I picked his smell up immediately and would have given chase if Helen hadn't called me back. She is such a spoilsport at times.

Yes, the actual source proved a bit of a disappointment, but it didn't stop Helen and Uncle John getting out their cameras and taking loads of pictures of the monument just to prove we had been there. Then we trotted on for about half a mile before turning back. All in all it was quite a good walk.

or Arkells 3B, which is a great brew, especially after a long walk, when you want something refreshing yet gutsy.

The walk

There are two different ways of reaching the source of the Thames from here, and both include hazards. The first is to turn left on leaving the pub and walk several hundred yards along the A433 until you reach a footpath sign. As this road is both narrow and particularly busy this can be a big problem if you are leading an excited dog that is hell-bent on beginning the walk.

If you take this footpath, you will simply follow the way signs for about half a mile, crossing a couple of fields until you come to the small monument declaring you have reached the Thames source.

I choose to take the second route, which begins at the back of the pub. You walk through a little wooden gate and into a small wooded area. This path is so well walked you will have no trouble spotting the track you have to follow. It leads to the railway line, which is fenced off.

You will reach a gate and stile which bring you to where the big hazard lies before you – this is where you have to cross the railway line.

It is not a busy track, but great care has to be taken as there are no flashing lights or warning bells. You just have to secure your dog on a tight lead, look both ways, then very, very carefully cross the track. Once over, you are in a field which leads to the Thames source. Just follow the well-worn path and you will come to the monument and a small circle of stones that indicate you have reached the source.

Most people are disappointed when they get here. 'Is this really it?' they say as they stare at the circle of stones. Can this really be where the mighty Thames begins its 154-mile journey to the North Sea? Surely not.

However, if you look deep into the ring of stones you may well note a few sporadic bursts of tiny bubbles making their way to the surface, which suggest this really could be the place you are looking for.

From thereon in, fields blend seamlessly together, offering a walk that will take you on to the Thames and Severn Canal and the Tunnel House Inn (see page 53). We walked on for half a mile, over a couple of fields, then turned and returned the way we had come as the lure of the Thames Head Inn drew us back.

The Swan Inn, Lechlade

The Swan is an apt name for this pub given the amazing number of swans you will encounter if you walk beside the river. I have never seen so many swans on one short river walk. Lechlade is an ancient market town 11 miles east of Cirencester and stands in the extreme south-east of Gloucestershire, close to the point where the rivers Coln and Leach flow into the Thames.

Some of the loveliest buildings in Lechlade are Georgian, and built from local stone – they have a glorious timeless feel that suggests that this town was once very wealthy. The Swan stands close to St Lawrence's Church, Burford Street. As it dates back to 1520 no doubt it would have provided food and shelter for those travelling on the stagecoaches that passed through the town en route to London.

It's a cosy, homely, country pub with a restaurant and bar area that fortunately have not been given a modern makeover as its charm lies in the fact that it has a really rural feel. The large fireplace that dominates the bar area is probably the only thing that has been extended recently, to provide more space for the many logs that are thrown on the fire.

Pythius is welcome here, but no one makes much fuss about the fact

Pythius says

This is the sort of country pub that border collies like because it's not posh and many of the customers are country folk. I feel comfortable here. As Helen says – it's cosy.

Had it not been for the fact that Helen and Auntie Liz got all poetic when they realised we were walking in Shelley's footsteps, this would go down as one of my favourite walks, as it offered everything I needed, including gallons and gallons of water. What's a dog to do when his mistress and auntie stand still and read out part of Shelley's poem which is carved on a stone plaque in the churchyard? When they get all poetical, it is a real pain. A similar thing happened when Helen and Auntie Kate visited Adlestrop.

Once we got to St John's lock and began to walk the riverbank they got less poetical as their attention was focused on me when all those swans began following us. I think they were scared I would have a go at them, or they would have a go at me, so we sort of ambled away from the river for a while. We were visiting in the winter, when there were no cattle in the fields, so I was able to run, but I believe that livestock use the fields the rest of the year, which means dogs have to be kept on a lead. Not good. As this walk has an enchanting ethereal beauty during the winter – why visit it in the summer? Sometimes a winter walk offers simply everything a dog could ask for. This one certainly does.

he is a dog. In fact he was not offered water when we called, but I am sure it would have been available had we asked, because this is a very friendly little pub. Nothing seemed too much trouble when we ordered lunch.

The food is basic pub grub, but the portions are generous and everything is hot, tasty and attractively served. I had the feeling that the person cooking my freshly battered haddock and chips had done so with great care. Real ale enthusiasts will not be disappointed with the range of brews on tap.

The walk

Lechlade offers serious walkers a chance to travel through three counties – Gloucestershire, Oxfordshire and Wiltshire – if they are prepared to take a five-mile circular walk. We chose a shorter circular amble that took just an hour to complete, and yet offered everything we asked for. We took the Shelley walk, so called because the poet Shelley visited Lechlade in 1815 while rowing from Windsor with his mistress Mary Godwin, her stepbrother Charles Clairmont and the novelist Thomas Love Peacocke. Their intention was to discover the source of the Thames – a quest they never realised as the river was so clogged with weeds at Inglesham that the local cattle were grazing on the riverbed.

During this trip the travellers spent a few leisurely days in Lechlade, which inspired Shelley to write his *A Summer Evening Churchyard*. The walk below is named after him. This is another of those delightful walks that calls for no instructions once you are headed in the right direction.

By following Shelley's walk through the churchyard and on through fields and a narrow hedge-lined lane flanked with water on either side, you will eventually reach the A417. Here it's time to put the dog on the lead, before turning right passing The Trout public house and over St John's Bridge, which was built in the 13th century and therefore one of the oldest bridges crossing the Thames.

There's a small gateway on the right once you have crossed the bridge. It leads to St John's lock, where you must keep the dog on the lead. It's here that you will discover a magnificent stone statue of Old Father Thames. This statue once stood at the head of the Thames at Trewsbury Mead, until it was vandalised in the 1970s. It seems very happy to be given pride of place at this attractive little lock. Once past the lock you are travelling on the Thames Path and heading for Ha'penny bridge, so called as it was once a toll bridge that charged people half a penny to cross.

This is the point where you meet all the swans, which seem so friendly; it is difficult to stop them following you along the path. Concerned that Pythius might decide to confront them, we guided him away from the riverbank and into the meadows, where several herons stood tall and still like majestic statues.

At the bridge you pass through the arch where steps will lead you to the road and back to the centre of Lechlade. One of the magic things about this walk is the way the magnificent spire of St Lawrence Church is never out of sight. To extend the walk, ignore the steps that lead to the road and back into the town and continue along the Thames Path.

The Victoria Arms, Marston

The Victoria Arms doesn't pretend to be a posh gastro-pub, it doesn't have to – people love it for what it is. Countless students, Oxford residents and tourists have made a pilgrimage over the years to the 'Vicky Arms', as it's called by those who know it well. Some come by punt and canoe, others walk the river footpath that begins at the University Parks, and some arrive by bike or car having made their way through Old Marston village. You approach the pub by taking a left turn down a winding country lane off the main road that runs through Old Marston. There are vicious road humps in place along this lane, so take it slowly; otherwise you will spend your time here waiting for the AA/RAC to help you get the undercarriage of your car sorted.

Outside the main door you will see a sign saying: BEEN WALKING THE DOG OR RAMBLING? PLEASE LEAVE THE OUTSIDE OUTSIDE AND REMOVE MUDDY BOOTS. THANK YOU.

This sign is actually saying two things, for whilst asking that you come in with clean feet, the sign also implies walkers and their canine friends are welcome.

Pythius and I have always been made very welcome here, although in the summer months when it gets very busy, we tend to sit outside in the garden that stretches down to the River Cherwell.

The Vicky Arms stands on the site of the old Marston Rope Ferry, which was the only way of getting from Marston to Headington to North Oxford and Summertown until the construction of the Marston Ferry link road was built.

The land and surrounding area is owned by the Oxford Preservation Trust, which buys up land surrounding Oxford to preserve it from the developers. This is why it has such a superb rural feel, despite being but a stone's throw from the city.

Pythius says

No one seems to take any notice of me when I walk into this pub; I am considered a customer with as many rights as Helen and Auntie Liz. I like that. Water is there should I need it, of course, but they don't make a big fuss about it.

This is a great walk, although Auntie Liz and Helen do get into a bit of a panic when we come to that busy road. I admit it is difficult to cross, but we always make it to the other side in the end. It's just a matter of being patient, not a virtue my mistress is known for! The river is deep and there are only a few inlets where I can splash about, but some of the streams leading into the river manage to keep me happy. There's loads of mud to wallow in too!

I am always amused when Helen makes her way over one particularly rickety wooden bridge that leads into the woods. She gets really scared as there are some planks missing and very little to grab hold of to steady herself. As this little bridge goes over a shallow stream, so shallow I cross without using the bridge, I don't know why she gets into such a panic. I guess she is scared of getting her beloved camera wet if she falls in. There are times when I think she's more concerned about that camera than she is about me! Why all the fuss I simply don't know, after all it is only a machine.

On a balmy summer's evening when the sky is bright you can sit in the pub garden and look out at the distant hills of Wytham Woods and enjoy watching the sun set. That is a magical moment.

In the summer you can order a jug of Pimms here, though Auntie Liz and I usually go for the beer, as a splendid assortment of real ales is always on tap. The selection of bottled ales is worth taking a look at too.

As for the food – well, if you enjoy home-cooked pub food with no frills, then you will be very happy with the menu. On Sundays, they serve a traditional Sunday roast, having acquired sirloin beef from the family butchers M. Feller, Son and Daughter of the Oxford covered market who sell organic meat.

Children are catered for but not with chicken nuggets. They get to choose something from the main menu that is served to them in small portions. Pensioners who don't want to face a large meal can make this choice too.

I always go for their fish and chips, as the batter is home made and the fish so fresh it tastes as if it has come straight from the sea that very day. The chips are good too!

By the way, readers into local history will be interested in the fact that we often sit at a table close to a sign which says that this is the spot where Oliver Cromwell sat in 1646 while waiting to liberate the city.

The walk

On leaving the Victoria Arms bear left, ignoring the pub's manicured garden, and head for a gap in the hedge by the car park, which will take you on a path through a coppice and alongside the Cherwell which flows into the centre of Oxford.

Take heed and please keep your dog on a lead whilst walking this path as it leads to the very busy B4495. At this point you have to be very patient and wait for a gap in the traffic, which is not easy during the rush hour. Once you have crossed the road, everything changes and a well-behaved dog can walk free, providing he is under control and obeys the country code.

You can't get lost on this walk; there are waymarkers at every point when a decision is required. There does come a moment when you have a choice: there are two ways through the first of the ancient unspoiled fields that are under the care of Wolfson College. Take either one, for they both end up leading you through another wooded area and back to the river path. Eventually you will arrive at the Rainbow Bridge on your right, which will take you into the University Parks. At this point, having travelled about a mile, we turn and head back for the Victoria Arms, but you can cross and walk the parks too, providing you keep your dog under tight control.

You will recognise the Rainbow Bridge instantly, as it's a beautifully designed curved footbridge built from concrete and metal in the shape of a rainbow – hence its name. It was constructed in the early 1920s as a project for the unemployed.

There are just two problems linked with this walk. The first is the mud that is often there during the summer months too. So wear mud-resistant boots and be prepared to get bogged down now and again. The second is the condition of the little wooden bridges you have to cross along the way; many are decaying rapidly, and are particularly slippery and unsafe in wet conditions.

The Fishes, North Hinksey

Once you leave the Botley Road (A420) that takes you into Oxford, and head south down North Hinksey Lane behind a large McDonald's, you will enter a part of Oxfordshire that hasn't changed in years. Suddenly you find yourself in a small pocket of West Oxford that seems as remote from the city as you can get.

Having passed a row of houses on the right of this lane, and the Manor house which looks rather like the higgledy-piggledy house that Jack built, you begin entering what is described as one of Oxford's green lungs. The unspoiled beauty of this area is due mostly to the Oxford Preservation Trust which, over the years, has secured the future of the fields and water meadows between Oxford and North Hinksey by purchasing this land before the developers could move in. We owe this trust a great deal.

Continue down North Hinksey Lane to a sharp corner with the 12th-century church of St Lawrence on your right. Bear to the left and you will come to the Fishes, an imposing Victorian red brick pub that has undergone several changes during the past decade, but is now in the safe hands of the Peach Pub Company, who also run the Fleece in Witney, whose motto is to only serve food to the public that they would be happy to serve themselves. The Fishes stands in three acres of wooded grounds leading to the Seacourt Stream, making it a great place to visit in the summer.

While working at *The Oxford Times* offices nearby, this was my local, as it was but a ten-minute walk away and they serve a jolly good working lunch here. I found the Fishes a great place to conduct interviews and meet up with my colleagues.

These days, this is one of the Oxford pubs that Pythius has come to appreciate, as he can now come along too. A bowl of water in the entrance tells you that this is a dog-friendly pub, and the staff's kindly attitude when you turn up with a canine

Pythius says

What a great pub, I love it. The staff are so well trained and professional and the food smells really delicious. There is always a bowl of chilled water outside the main door, and one is offered when I go inside in case I need more. I love the buzz – this pub is always busy, filled with discerning people enjoying themselves. Many give me a pat as they pass our table. That's nice.

All the stiles on this walk have a friendly dog-hole which enables me to crawl straight through, but humans are not quite so lucky. One stile proved so high when we walked this way last autumn, poor Auntie Liz ended up having to crawl through the dog-hole too!

Then there was the problem with the travellers' barking dogs, who frightened me so much, I ran the other way. They were penned up close to the path that skirts the rear of the *Oxford Times* offices (the newspaper press is housed in a gigantic cream building which you simply can't miss as it dominates the landscape). I don't think they should have been there, but as their barks were really ferocious, I didn't stop to investigate, nor did Auntie Liz and Helen.

As there are loads of lovely little streams running through these water meadows, I always enjoy this walk, though I am not allowed to wander too far in case I disturb the wildlife.

friend says the rest. Dogs are certainly welcome here.

The décor is stylish and modern, and the conservatory extension, which looks out on the garden and stream, is an ideal place to be when it is just not quite warm enough to sit out in the garden. If the weather is good, you can order a picnic basket that comes complete with rugs to sit on, and enjoy your lunch while lazing beside the stream. This is something that Pythius and I often do during high summer.

The Peach Pub Company prides itself on serving seasonal local food, and a menu which has been created by not just the chefs, but the waiting staff too. In the summer months, most of the fruit and vegetables featured on the menu come from nearby Medley Manor Farm's Pick-Your-Own in Binsey and are often delivered by Charles Gee, who loads up his bicycle basket with freshly harvested goodies such as asparagus and pedals over to the Fishes. You can't get much greener or fresher than that! The fish menu is worth taking seriously too as the Peach Pub Company is signed up to the Scottish Fisherman's Scheme which ensures maximum traceability and freshness of fish. It also means you never know what fish will feature as the special of the day.

The walk

There are footpath signs both sides of the pub. Retrace your steps on leaving, cross the steep cobbled bridge just past the church and you can walk a delightfully tree-lined path known as Willow Walk that links with the Osney Mead trading estate. Or turn left on leaving the pub, and just 100 yards down the road you can take a footpath on the left which leads into 33 acres of lush water meadows within the Oxford Flood Plain and the Green Belt, which was purchased by the Oxford Preservation Trust in 1997.

The land is now managed as part of the Upper Thames Environmentally Sensitive Area. Dogs must be kept under control while walking this area. Posted on the gate and stile which leads to this walk is a map indicating the footpaths you can take, which will lead you to nearby South Hinksey or allow you to simply enjoy the meadows and make up your own circular walk.

One word of warning: the wooden stiles, which must have been erected some time ago, are now showing severe signs of wear and tear. Some are rotting and others are particularly slippery. Do be careful; these are not stiles that can be leapt over in a single bound.

The cottage opposite the entrance to this walk bears a blue plaque dedicated to the 19th-century artist and critic John Ruskin, who admired the rustic charm of this area. In 1874, he thought up a scheme which would provide Oxford undergraduates with the benefits of manual labour and at the same time improve condition of Hinksey villages by building a road that would link North Hinksey with South Hinksey. If you ignore the footpaths for a moment and continue up the lane past the Fishes, you will come to the point where his road ends abruptly, when the students' enthusiasm for manual labour began to wane.

The Woodman Inn,
North Leigh

You will find the Woodman Inn in New Yatt Road, North Leigh, off the A4095 about four miles from Witney. It's one of those delightful country pubs that does not pretend to be posh. It's a real pub in every sense of the world as it's there for both residents of the village and real ale enthusiasts who attend the regular beer festivals held there throughout the year. Look up this pub in the *Good Beer Guide* and you will discover that CAMRA members speak very highly of it, as this is a pub which takes real ale seriously.

The first beer festival of the year usually takes place during the Easter holidays; others follow throughout the year. As there are usually more than 20 different themed beers on offer during these festivals, all of which can be tasted in a marquee erected at the rear of the pub, these festivals attract a great following. Even during mid-week, the range of real ales available is impressive – at least three are on tap at any given time.

Pythius enjoys visiting this pub, although he seldom calls in during the beer festivals as he doesn't like crowds. He prefers an early evening visit during the summer when the bar staff can give him their full attention, often offering him a Bonio biscuit or two, which they keep hidden behind the bar for their canine visitors.

The Woodman has a homely feel. Traditional chunky tables and chairs fill the wood-trimmed bar, with its wood flooring and blackboard menu. Very few pieces of bric-a-brac clutter the walls and surfaces – they are not needed. Vases of fresh flowers are usually placed around the bar and a large potted tree in one corner of the room adds the necessary touches needed to bring it to life.

The menu is best described as an honest pub menu with no frills. Local food does make up most of the menu, which is cooked to order at a very reasonable price, but this pub doesn't boast about using local meat and vegetables. Here local food is considered the norm.

Dishes such as Welsh rarebit, doorstep sandwiches and chip butties are also listed for those who just want a bar snack, which can be enjoyed with a selection of local mustards from nearby Shaken Oak Farm.

Pythius says

It's not just the Bonios that attract me to this pub; it's the people who run it. When this pub boasts that it's dog-friendly, they are telling the truth. It really is dog-friendly; all sorts of dogs pop in for a quick drink with their owners during early evening. On entering, I am greeted by name, patted on the head, offered a bowl of water and then invited to sit wherever I please. Those enjoying a pint usually greet me too. What more could a dog could ask for?

When a walk offers me a stream, a river and a common where I can run free, I ask for nothing more. This walk offers all those things. I admit there was a rather scary moment Helen hasn't really admitted to when, on following the stream past the farm buildings, we arrived at a metal gate that was keeping a herd of inquisitive bullocks in place. After much rustling of paper as she and Uncle John (who had joined us on this walk) referred to their maps, they finally realised they were on the wrong side of the stream and had to jump from boulder to boulder in order to cross it. Having placed the stream on their right once more (they had crossed a small bridge without realising it, because they were chattering too much), all was well.

Of course, I knew they had missed the little bridge, but they never take any notice of me. The path to the road thereafter is rather narrow, and Helen is right, it's frequently used by horses, so be very, very careful at this point. Once you arrive at the Common, having been placed on a lead while travelling the road (not good), everything changes and you will be allowed to run free. And by free, I do mean free. It's simply amazing. Here is a wild space where dogs can run and run and run in any direction and, in the end, reach the river where willows drop their branches into the water, and kingfishers fly backwards and forwards on a summer day. Paradise!

The walk

There are so many walks and footpaths in the North Leigh area; walkers are spoiled for choice. My favourite, when time permits, takes in another village and another pub. It's a six-mile circular walk that begins at the local church about quarter of a mile away and takes the walker to Stonesfield and back.

I usually drive from the pub to the starting point, which can be found by turning right on leaving the Woodman, then left down Church Road until you arrive at the village hall and car park which stands opposite the 11th-century church of St Mary. It's a safe place to park.

Beside the church you will find a hard track leading to a farm and open countryside. When you see a metal gate on your right, take this track which leads you downhill to another gate.

The path eventually comes to a lane: turn left and look for a path on your right which is the drive to Holly Court Farm, taking you past farm buildings, dilapidated barns and a superb hand-crafted tree house. On your right is a fast-flowing stream. Keep that stream to your right or you will end up in a meadow that may be filled with bullocks. The path narrows now, and be warned: it can become very muddy at times. Hoof marks in the mud indicate that horses use it frequently, so it's best to keep the dog close at hand to avoid dog and riders meeting head on.

You will eventually come to a single-track road. Turn right, having placed the dog on a lead, cross a bridge over the River Evenlode and up the hill, crossing another bridge over a railway line where you turn right and follow the lane. Soon you will encounter a metal gate on your right on which a large white sign referring to Section 34 of the Road Traffic Act is placed, telling you that motor vehicles are not permitted on common land.

Some joker has shot a few bullets into the sign, obliterating the date of the regulation, so you can't mistake it. This is the gate your dog has been waiting for, as you have now reached what locals call Stonesfield Common (see the view below), though none of my maps gives it this name.

The view is breathtaking as you are standing on high ground. Below, the River Evenlode gently meanders through the landscape and woods begin to appear on your right. You can walk left, right or simply go forward – well-worn paths in the grass formed by countless footsteps will show you the way. If you go straight on, you will eventually reach the river, where someone has thoughtfully placed a large log, to enable walkers to sit and linger should they wish. I certainly linger here, if only to see if I can spot a kingfisher. Once rested, take the uphill path to the left of the footbridge (you are walking on Akeman Street at this point, its terrace cut into the hillside two thousand years ago), past banks of wild marjoram, keeping the hedgerow on your right, until you arrive at the outskirts of Stonesfield. A left-hand sign indicating the Oxfordshire Way will take you to The Ridings and the White Horse pub, known for its home-cooked food. Dogs are permitted into the bar, but not the restaurant. Having stopped off for a refreshing pint of Old Hooky, you can return the way you came, adding a few changes by taking a different path across the common.

To visit the nearby Roman villa foundations and mosaic, instead of taking the path back up the common, cross the footbridge and follow the track across the fields and the railway for three-quarters of a mile till you see the villa on your left. From the villa take the path by the entrance gate up through some lovely woods until you come to East End: turn left along the road for a couple of hundred yards and look for the path on the right that returns you to North Leigh.

The Wheatsheaf Inn, Northleach

When I first began taking Pythius out for a pub lunches followed by a walk, I asked friends which pubs I should aim for. The advice given by one friend has always held me in good stead. I was told to go for the most stylish pub in town as such establishments nearly always welcome dogs, providing you are prepared to eat in the bar. Pick a small, scruffy little pub and they will probably turn you away. I have stuck to this rule and seldom been disappointed.

The rule certainly applies at the Wheatsheaf Inn, Northleach, a 17th-century coaching inn, built in Cotswold stone, which is situated on the right-hand side of the main road as you approach from Burford.

Northleach is a thriving little town, often referred to as a Cotswold secret, as it's tucked well away from the busy A40. Midway between Oxford and Cheltenham, or Stow-on-the-Wold and Cirencester, it stands at the crossroads of the Roman Fosse Way. This ancient town, with its unspoiled market place which has changed little since the 15th century, is rich in architectural delights, including half-timbered Tudor houses, merchants' houses and even a house of correction which was built in the 18th century.

Its church, St Peter and St Paul, which dates from the 12th century, is certainly worth a visit as it bears witness to the wealth that the highly prized Cotswold wool once brought to Northleach.

If you are lucky, you will find a parishioner on duty in the church who will willingly act as a volunteer guide should you wish to know more about the architecture. The story behind the pig's head and cat and fiddle carved from stone which hang in the porch is fascinating and it's good to learn more about the many impressive memorial brasses on the floor that pay homage to rich wool traders and their wives of bygone times.

Because the Wheatsheaf has been refurbished recently, it's difficult to describe the interior. With flagstone and wooden flooring, modern high back chairs, wooden window shutters and white walls, it falls midway between rustic and stylish modern. The three inter-connecting areas (two restaurant spaces and the bar area) give a spacious feel. The

Pythius says

Well I was certainly made welcome. Almost too welcome actually. The moment I walked in several of the young serving staff rushed over to give me a pat on the head. Whilst this was all very impressive, there are only so many pats a border collie can cope with. But it was kindly meant, so I guess I couldn't complain, especially as I was allowed to place my paws under the table in the dinning area. All very posh actually, so I stayed under the table, so as not to upset anyone or trip the waitress up while she was carrying food. Several of the customers leaned over to say hello while I was there. That was nice but I stayed firmly where I was, because that's what I've been trained to do when I'm allowed in a posh dining room.

How I loved darting in and out of that tiny river. It was so clean. I have never seen such a clean river! It smelt lovely too, which pleased Helen, because it meant she didn't have to put up with a smelly dog stinking of muddy river water when we travelled home in the car. We did encounter one small snag on the day we did this walk... cows. These beautiful big bovine beasts sat there chewing the cud whilst looking me over suspiciously. Helen kept me on the lead at that point, which curtailed my sense of freedom until we got to the dog-friendly stile. Having left the cows behind, I was able to rush around once more discovering some fantastic new smells. She and Auntie Liz took it in turns to stay outside with me when we got to the church, so that they could explore this wonderful old building.

few ornaments and pictures on the walls are linked with horse racing, presumably reflecting the fact that it is owned and run by the Champion family.

Pythius was certainly made to feel welcome; he was even allowed to eat in the restaurant area, which suited him perfectly. The menu is extensive with many delicious options listed including a magnificent choice of freshly-cut doorstep sandwiches, home-made soup and delicious upmarket specials such as crispy duck served on a bed of red currants with a red currant and thyme sauce, or garlic and herb-roasted pork tenderloin. Oxfordshire ales such as Old Hooky are on tap, and bowls of cold water are available for canine visitors.

The walk

Leave the Wheatsheaf, turn left and make for the Market Place, and then head towards the church. Now turn left into a narrow road by The Wool House and then right towards College Row. At this point, a small path called Layton Lane leads to the Playing Field. Turn towards the tennis court and you will discover the beginnings of the River Leach on your left. Pythius had a great time splashing about in its glistening waters where clusters of wild watercress grow alongside the bank. We finally pulled him away from the river and by keeping the tennis courts to our left, crossed the grass diagonally to reach a kissing gate by the hedge. We then took a sharp right and climbed straight up the hill until we reached a stile that is fitted with a dog gate.

At this point turn and take in a fine view of Northleach and the valley below, before carrying on uphill along the field boundary. Keep this boundary on your right until you reach Helen's Ditch and find yourself on a grassy bridle track. Now turn right as the track leads towards the centre of town. By taking a small path on the left as you approach the town, you can spend a while visiting the church, returning to the Market Place by taking the right hand path through the churchyard. The whole trip took us about an hour, because we took time out for Pythius to splash about in the river, but most people could do this walk in under 40 minutes.

The Fox Inn, Lower Oddington

The Fox Inn, with its flagstone floors and creeper-clad building, dates back to the 11th century. It stands in the centre of a lovely Cotswold village that can be reached by taking the A424 from Burford to Stow-on-the-Wold, and then a right turn to Icomb: it is signposted from there. Although it is well known for its superb Norman church with its awe-inspiring doom wall painting, which was restored early in the 20th century, having been virtually abandoned for many years, Lower Oddington is not a tourist destination. Perhaps it should be as it boasts one of the best pubs for miles around.

The Fox is one of those country pubs that American visitors dream about as it offers everything, particularly atmosphere, which is generated in part by its very hard-working landlord who is not afraid to knuckle down and help serve food and clear tables.

As country pubs go, it really is in a class all of its own, as it is both comfortable and dependable. The variety of real ale on offer is impressive and the food, which is locally sourced and all cooked on the premises, is outstanding. This is one of those remarkable pubs that never lets you down. The welcome is just as warm in the winter as the summer and the quality of food never wavers.

Pythius loves this pub because they treat him with the respect a border collie demands. Water is always available if he needs it, but it is never forced on him. And if customers coming in after a five-mile walk call for water to quench their thirst before lunch, it arrives promptly in a glistening metallic jug overflowing with ice cubes.

Pythius enjoys sitting out in the attractive little garden at the rear, but he is equally welcome inside providing we have booked a table. Table bookings are essential as this pub is always busy, especially during Sunday lunch times when a succulent traditional roast with all the trimmings is always on the menu.

This is the pub I visit with my friend Kate and her black labrador Polly. We use it as a starting point for a walk through Adlestrop, which is but a mile away. Do you remember Adlestrop? Most people do, thanks to poet Edward Thomas who immortalised this lovely village with his poem describing that day in late June when the express train once drew up there unwontedly. Sadly the railway station and the bare platform he

Pythius says

I like this pub. How could one fail to like an establishment that treats dogs with as much respect as it does its customers? Polly and I always walk in together, exhausted from a long cross-country walk, taken at a sprightly pace as Kate strides ahead like no one else I know; Polly and I follow, with Helen bringing up the rear. When we arrive at the Fox we are all exhausted and grateful to be allowed to place our paws under the table, without further interruption.

Auntie Kate is so good at organising walks that I always relax when I am out with her. She knows how to look after dogs too, always looking ahead in case there is a hazard that calls for me and Polly to be put on our leads quickly.

This walk is good as it is mostly open bridleways and footpaths with the occasional wood to keep Polly and me amused. The only thing we have to look out for are those frightfully posh horses, and when I say posh I do mean posh. They are quite friendly though, often leaning their heads over the fence to say hello as we pass. Kate always stops to talk to them, the rest of us go on, confident that she will catch us up easily when she has a mind to. When we get to Adlestrop, Polly and I have to stand still and be good while Helen and Kate read out the Adlestrop poem once more. I don't know what all the fuss is about actually; it's just a silly old poem about a train stopping and birds singing. But they seem to like it, so who am I to argue? As this is quite a long walk by Helen's standards, I admit to being glad to turn the corner and see that lovely pub waiting for us.

observed in 1914 are no longer there. Only the station sign 'Adlestrop' now hangs proudly over one of the original railway benches in the bus shelter. But that doesn't prevent Kate and me from paying homage to both poet and poem when walking in this area. I suspect that many visitors taking lunch at the Fox also take this walk to a much-loved memorial of a railway station long gone, but certainly not forgotten.

The walk

If you take in both Adlestrop and Daylesford this walk will take at least two hours, though under Kate's command we often do it in less. It's a circular walk so you can begin or end at Adlestrop. If you want to keep Adlestrop until last, take the first left turn after leaving the pub (just before the post box) along a lane sign posted St Nicholas Church. Do spare a moment to visit the church and take a look at the doom painting and the beautiful Jacobean pulpit – you will not be disappointed.

There's a gravel track now; just follow that path across a field or two. The path eventually veers to the right, which leads to a small field and footbridge over the River Evenlode. You will now cross another field to a gateway and a bridge over the railway lines which are still used by the express trains. Now keep the hedge on your left until you reach the road.

Turn left into Daylesford, stopping off to browse round Daylesford Organics if you want to delight your taste buds. Pass New Farm, then take the footpath sign which will take you to the Dell, a disused quarry and Daylesford Hill Farm. At this point you will wonder if you are allowed to walk on, as the path takes you right through the centre of the farm. Actually you can walk on, footpath rules permit this, but as there are horses in this yard it is advisable to put the dog on a lead until you get out the other side. Now you will travel through some charming woods and on until you reach the A346 again.

At this point you can follow the signpost to Adlestrop and then Oddington, or do as Kate does and march out into open country, adding another mile or two to this idyllic walk. She does this by turning right at a footpath marker just a quarter of a mile on after crossing the A346. There are so many footpaths to choose from once you strike out in this direction. You could make for Adlestrop Hill, or walk to Coomb Wood – the choice is yours – just remember that there will come a moment when you will want to turn and take in Adlestrop and return to Oddington. The last time Kate and I shared this walk with our dogs it was late spring. Never have I walked through such beautiful well-kept countryside. The many well-groomed racehorses with their gleaming coats and sparkling eyes that you pass along the way act as a constant reminder that this is a wealthy area, where hand-crafted wooden gates all open easily, hedges are well trimmed and all the stiles are easy to use.

The Turf Tavern, Oxford

Even people who haven't visited Oxford's famous Turf Tavern may be familiar with its interior, as this is the bar where TV's Inspector Morse and his loyal sidekick Lewis downed a few companionable pints while discussing – and sometimes solving – their latest complicated case. Tucked away beside the city wall, the Turf is one of Oxford's oldest and most atmospheric pubs. You find it by leaving Catte Street, passing under Hertford College's Bridge of Sighs and turning left down St Helen's Passage, which was originally known as Hell Passage because it was once so squalid.

Although The Turf Tavern dates back to the 14th century, most of the present building with its low ceilings, gnarled beams and small interconnecting rooms was built in the 16th century.

In the summer you can sit in the beer garden if it is too crowded inside. In the winter glowing braziers are lit in the little courtyard to keep those drinking outside warm and snug, which is probably one of many reasons why it's so popular with students, particularly in the cold weather.

Originally named the Spotted Cow, the Turf changed its name in 1842. It is thought it was named after a nearby gambling hall where turf accountants met. I don't take Pythius to the city often, but when we do pay a visit, we always make for this pub, as dogs are very welcome here.

There's an extensive menu of hot meals and sandwiches available at modest prices, which are best described as basic pub grub dishes. That's OK by me; they are freshly cooked and served promptly by an army of cheerful young people who always appear to be enjoying their work.

These young servers know their beers too. Enquire about any one of the many ever-changing guest beers that are on tap here, and you will find the staff can usually describe their flavour with both enthusiasm and knowledge (perhaps that's because most of the staff are students attending the University?).

Because the Turf is very busy at times, Pythius and I make for a corner table where he can tuck himself out of reach of the many young feet marching through the bar. There are usually bowls of cold water left outside for visiting canines, so that he can satisfy his thirst before going in.

Pythius says

I rather enjoy tucking myself away under the table at this pub and listening to the chatter all around me. It's like nothing I usually hear. Amid the student laughter I get to hear people discussing deep philosophic problems and all sorts of learned things. I can't say I understand what they are saying, of course, but I do like listening to the long words they use. I'm convinced that if we stayed long enough I would get to know who Aristotle and Plato are. Sitting by the brazier in the winter is fun too, especially during the Christmas holidays when everyone congregates at the Turf for a glass of warmed mulled wine. Dogs like me enjoying being snuggled up with a gathering of young people now and again.

Being kept on the lead for the entire walk is not my idea of fun, but as Helen said previously, I do accept this is necessary when we visit Oxford and the University Parks.

Besides, there are so many families, mothers pushing prams and student joggers using the paths that twist in and out of the flower beds that I need to be close to Helen. I wouldn't like to get lost in the big city.

Nevertheless, there are many pleasant things about this walk. People often stop and smile at me and call me 'nice doggie'. Sometimes they tap me on the head and talk to Helen at the same time, because Oxford is a very friendly place. She often bumps into people she knows too, which is nice. It gives her a chance to chat and let them see what a terrific dog I am. Obviously, she always clutches a plastic bag while walking the parks just in case I need to make an unexpected toilet stop.

The walk

If you turn right on leaving the Turf, and go via Bath Place, rather than Helen's Passage, walk into Holywell Street and turn left, you will find yourself walking towards the Bodleian Library. Cross the road at the traffic lights by the King's Arms (the pub on the corner) and you will be in Parks Road.

Follow Parks Road for about a quarter of a mile, passing the Natural History Museum on your right and Keble College on your left. Keble is Oxford's only red brick college, so you won't miss it. Keep walking for a moment or two and you will discover the first of two gates into the University Parks on your right. These gates are open from 8 am until half an hour before dusk every day except Christmas Eve. They lead to 70 acres of well-tended parkland with superb herbaceous displays and a further four acres of land that lies between the upper and lower levels of the River Cherwell, traditionally known as Mesopotamia – the Greek for 'between the rivers'.

If you wander along the various paths you will eventually discover a circular lily pond and the High Bridge, also known as the Rainbow Bridge. By crossing this bridge you can follow a footpath along the River Cherwell (which is a tributary of the River Thames) – see page 105 for the Victoria Arms and details of this walk.

We tend to stay in the parks and walk paths that take us past clusters of mature trees and beautiful borders planted with the most amazing assortment of shrub, trees and flowers. Unfortunately Pythius has to be kept on his lead, but he seems to accept that this is necessary when we visit Oxford.

The Royal Oak, Ramsden

Ramsden stands in a shallow valley on the north-eastern fringes of the Cotswolds, just four miles from Witney. There was a time when this unspoiled little village lay deep within the ancient Forest of Wychwood. It's thought the land on which it stands was one of the first parts of the forest to be cleared for settlement.

It's a tranquil village, peopled with families who can trace their ancestors back through the centuries. Some of its residents still work on the farms surrounding the village as their forebears did.

In the centre of Ramsden, close to the modern war memorial and church, stands the Royal Oak, an atmospheric 17th-century inn that boasts exposed Cotswold stone walls, low beams, shining brass and a great choice of real ales.

Everyone loves this pub, particularly dogs, as they are made welcome in the bar area or the little patio garden outside. Well-behaved children are welcomed too.

This is one of those friendly country pubs that offers you a welcome the moment you open the door. Visitors are never in doubt that this pub is special. During the winter months, dancing flames of a roaring log fire illuminate the room, adding to the warmth of welcome.

As it has gained an entry in CAMRA's *Good Beer Guide* since 1991, people don't just come to the Royal Oak for the food. They know the beer is jolly good too and the wine list is particularly impressive.

Lovers of British food will be happy to know that local produce features large on the menu. Lamb, eggs, fruit and vegetables from nearby farms are used wherever possible. Local prize-winning mustards, created just a couple of miles away by Bruce Young of Shaken Oak Farm, are also incorporated into various dishes.

Indeed, the Royal Oak is now a gastropub of some repute. There is a light lunch menu for those who don't need a full meal, but most go for the glorious meals on the main lunch or dinner menu and make their visit here a real occasion. A lunch at the Royal Oak is not something that should be hurried. So enjoy the walk first, then sit back and relax while the dog sleeps it off under the table.

Pythius says

This pub is always crowded, which can be difficult for a dog trying to manoeuvre his way through all those legs to reach the spot where canines are allowed. However, as I am always made welcome, I guess all that anxiety is worth it. The food certainly smells scrumptious, though I never get to taste any. As lots of Helen's friends use this pub, lunch here is usually a very sociable affair.

Helen let me off the lead the moment we had passed the first stile, which gave me the freedom to follow the path Mr Fox uses. He left loads of markers which I would have loved to have investigated further, but knowing Helen would get mad if I rolled in his deliciously smelly calling cards, I curbed my canine instincts.

How I loved the copse – so many intense smells – perfect for a dog. Not necessarily good for humans though. The moment we were in, I could tell the atmosphere disturbed Helen, so did that gloriously muddy pond in the centre all covered with slime and weeds. Perhaps that's a story that's best not told. Though, if I'm honest, I think she overreacted. I didn't get that dirty. Besides, what's the matter with a bit of mud when you are out in the open air? Most of it had rubbed off by the time we got back to the pub.

The walk

On leaving the pub, turn left and head up Wilcote Lane, until you come to a notice in front of woods which tells you not to enter. To the left you will notice a gate, then a wooden stile and a footpath sign marked Wychwood Way. Once you have found this path, it's just a matter of following the waymarkers which in a couple of hundred yards take you past a fenced-off wood on the right and open fields on the left. When Pythius and I did this walk, we followed the Wychwood Way for a mile or so into Holly Grove, quite a spooky wood and often muddy, with evidence of the ancient practice of coppicing.

Returning through Holly Grove the way we had come, we walked up the lane into Wilcote. We ventured over a wooden stile opposite the church which bore a footpath sign pointing into a copse. As the copse is dark, dense and rather muddy in parts, with overhanging tangled branches tickling our heads, I wished we had just walked on. There was something distinctly disturbing about the way the thick foliage of the trees and their twisted trunks bore down on intruders.

I think at this point it's best to warn those who own water-loving

dogs that there's a very murky pool in the centre of the copse...

In Wilcote other footpath markers offered us the chance to go further if we crossed the road. We could have also taken a path to Topples Wood, or another to The Plough Inn, which Pythius knows well (see page 86). He would have like that, but we followed the path past the muddy pool, crossed a stile into a field, turned left and followed the path back to Ramsden, stopping every now and again to admire the rural landscape that lay before us and listen to the silence, broken only by occasional birdsong.

The wonderful thing about this walk, which took us less than an hour, is the constant choice of footpaths open to walkers who wish to go further. We could have followed paths that would have taken us to Finstock, North Leigh or into Wychwood Forest, or explored the walled and gated fertility well marked on the Ordnance Survey map as Lady Well. Because these ancient routes are used regularly, it's really a matter of following well-trodden paths, map in hand.

The Rose and Crown, Shilton

Many years ago, a young man leaving the Rose and Crown was seen trying to rake the reflection of a full moon from the village pond believing it to be a cheese, and so the term 'Silly Shilton' was coined. However, there is nothing silly about Shilton, or the people who live there. It's a tranquil, unspoiled Cotswold village tucked away in the quiet Shill Brook valley, just below the busy A40 and but a mile from Carterton, and the people who live there are very kindly folk.

The Shill Brook runs through the centre of the village creating a ford by the duck pond, which has to be crossed if you want to take the short route to Carterton. The Rose and Crown, which stands alongside the main road, is pretty good too. On balmy sunny days, there is nothing nicer than sitting in its rustic little garden at the rear enjoying a pint of ale in the shade of its apple trees. This is another pub that takes local produce seriously and prides itself on serving home-cooked food.

Much of their meat comes from nearby Foxbury Farm, which makes award-winning sausages from Gloucester Old Spot pork, which are simply delicious. Their steaks (also from the farm) are also sumptuous. In the winter, a roaring log fire warms the small bar area where dogs are invited to place their paws under the table. Pythius certainly enjoys the fuss that the locals make of him when visiting here. Because this pub stands in dog-walking territory, dogs are frequent visitors.

The walk

Had a Shilton resident not explained where this walk started, I admit we might never have found the entrance as the waymarker is covered with foliage and it points to what appears to be the garden of a private house. You will find the marker opposite the village's stone-built pump, a short distance from the pub if you turn right. If you turn your back to the pump and look carefully, you will see that the footpath travels down the side of the house and then to a stile and open country.

This is a well-worn path that if taken in its entirety will lead you to Burford two miles away. We usually just go half way, then turn back as the view on the return is just as lovely as the one encountered on the outward walk. This is undulating countryside at its very best; breath-

---

Pythius says

Yes, this is a very friendly little pub. Everyone makes a fuss of me when I come here, which is nice. And although I am welcome in the bar area, we usually end up sitting in the garden to enjoy the peaceful nature of this place.

There's just one snag unfortunately – Shilton is only a few miles from Brize Norton's military airbase. This means that the silence Helen enjoys so much is brutally interrupted every now and then by the roar of aircraft engines. Because Shilton is so close to the base, these aircraft are flying quite low when they go over the pub garden. I was certainly quite alarmed when I first experienced this noise.

Helen's right – the countryside you encounter on this walk is very beautiful, peaceful too when the aircraft are not flying overhead. However, despite that, I have to say it is not my favourite walk, as I am kept on a lead for a considerable part of the way. Given all the wonderful smells I would far rather be running round and round, sniffing out Mr Fox and running after rabbits. But she says 'no' and no it is.

Naturally, I find the stone stiles easy – just one big jump and I am over; no problem for me at all. However, they really could prove a problem for older or overweight dogs who have not been trained to jump and are not as slim-line and clever as I am.

---

takingly beautiful, actually. All the stiles are built of stone, with large stone slabs in the centre. Because Pythius was trained for agility jumps when he was young, he finds them no problem, but some dogs might have difficulties.

Signs along the walk inform walkers that this is a conservation area and wildlife must be respected, so once we get past the first field, we usually put Pythius on his lead. There are waymarkers at every stile and the walk takes you straight along the side of fields, until the land dips and you arrive at a marvellous green space fringed with woods. It's a wonderful sight, particularly as the crystal clear waters of Shill Brook ripple gently alongside the woods. We stop here for a while to take in the lush surroundings, listen to the birds and simply enjoy being in the middle of the most remarkable countryside; then, once Pythius has had a drink in the brook, we head back, having walked our mile. Burford lies just another mile down the track.

The Queen's Head, Stow-on-the-Wold

The Queen's Head is one of the most dog-friendly pubs in the Cotswolds. The day Auntie Liz, Pythius and I arrived, I went on ahead to check that we would all be welcome. I needn't have bothered; two dogs were already sitting comfortably under the table while their masters enjoyed a pint or two of the local brew from nearby Donnington Brewery. By the time we were ready to leave, a further four dogs had joined the throng and we bumped into another two entering as we were going out.

The Queen's Head stands in the middle of the Market Square. If you are lucky you may be able to spot a spare place near the pub to park your car. If not, follow the signposts to the public car park which is only a few minutes' walk from the main shopping area and the many enchanting little shops which give this Cotswold town so much character.

Like so many old pubs we have visited over the years it's rather dark when you first enter. Like us, you may find yourself blinking when you first walk in for despite the fact that the ceilings are not that low and the windows appear large enough to let in sufficient light, they don't. This experience only lasts a moment or two however.

Once your eyes have adjusted you discover that you have entered a comfortable old bar bedecked with dried hops and simply buzzing with life. Both locals and tourists flock to this 17th-century pub, which rates as one of the most friendly places we have visited. There's a second bar and a small restaurant at the back, also a small courtyard overflowing with attractive colourful hanging baskets and tubs of flowers.

The menu offers standard pub fare: ham, egg and chips, steak and ale pie and bangers and mash, which is attractively served and arrives piping hot within moments of giving your order. Water is available for canine friends if required.

Pythius says

This is certainly a dog-friendly pub. While Helen and Auntie Liz munched their way through a couple of home-made steak and kidney pies and chips, I had a good old chat with all the other dogs who had tucked their paws under the tables. There were more dogs in this pub than any other we have visited. Some were visitors like me. I got on well with them, but some were regulars who guarded their territory with low warning growls when I ventured too close.

This walk worked for me, as I was able to run free once we had crossed that dreadful road. Actually there was so much traffic rushing through that it really frightened me. Thank goodness Helen had my lead held tight so that I couldn't move until she did. There are times when a large field which gives me space to run is all I need, particularly when Helen has remembered to bring a ball that I can chase.

The walk

On the advice of friends who visit this area often we did not seek out a long country walk, but made for the cricket field, which stands across the main A429 that runs through the town. This is a very busy road, so we had to wait some time before we could cross safely. You reach this road by taking the small passageway to the left of the Queen's Head when you leave. All you have to do once you have crossed the road is go straight, straight, straight, until you find yourself in a glorious field where the dog can run free.

Pythius loved it, he ran and ran, chasing the ball we threw for him and then occasionally stopping to admire the view, before giving the ball his full attention once more. The surrounding fields were filled with sheep when we visited in the summer, so we stayed where we were and just enjoyed the space. It's certainly the largest cricket field we have ever visited, and the views from the bottom of the field are stunning.

The Swan, Swinbrook

The Swan was singled out by *The Good Pub Guide* as the Oxfordshire Dining Pub of the Year 2009, which is a very important accolade. All pubs in this guide are there by merit, having been nominated by members of the public and then inspected by the guide officials.

You will discover the Swan nestling besides the River Windrush on

the edge of Swinbrook, an unspoiled little Cotswold village two miles east of Burford. It's all very picturesque. Indeed, the walks in this area are renowned for their beauty. Pythius certainly enjoys visiting the Swan, which boasts that it is very dog-friendly on its website where you will find a picture of the pub-dog Boysie as he walks arrogantly through the bar.

The owner of this pub is Her Grace, The Dowager Duchess of Devonshire, Deborah Mitford, the youngest of the six Mitford sisters. When she refurbished the Swan recently, with the help of landlord Archie Orr-Ewing and his wife Nicola, she decorated all the walls with large black and white prints of family photographs that had never been on show before. These include pictures of Diana, who married Oswald Mosley, Unity, who became obsessed with Hitler, and Nancy, who wrote *Love in a Cold Climate*. These pictures certainly add an intriguing touch to its small adjoining rooms, which are all comfortably appointed.

I had better warn you that this pub is so popular that finding somewhere to park at the weekend can be difficult. You may discover its small car park is full, and end up leaving your car on the narrow approach road.

It goes without saying that the food served here is scrumptious. Most items on the menu are sourced locally, including Aberdeen Angus beef that comes from a nearby family farm and game from the Barrington estate. I have eaten here frequently and never once been disappointed.

The beer is fine too. Archie treats the real ales he serves with the respect they deserve. Organic lager from the Cotswold Organic Lager Company is on tap too.

The walk

If there aren't any cattle in the first field, we normally take the footpath that begins opposite the pub. It allows us to follow the Windrush across a couple of fields to Asthall. It's a gentle walk and only about two miles there and back.

I call it our kingfisher walk, because we have often spotted a sparkling flash of blue feathers dart into the river. Those are magic, never-to-be-forgotten moments, and part of the charm of walking this undulating landscape which has hardly changed over the centuries.

The first stile is constructed out of a large slab of local stone, which Pythius leaps in one bound, but smaller dogs may find it difficult. Once

Pythius says

Yes – this is a great pub. Over the years Helen has brought all her dogs here, including the great dog Apollo who lived with her before me. Her first dog Fred, who was also a border collie, loved this pub too – so Helen says.

And why not, it's all very comfortable and friendly, although I wish that Boysie, the pub-dog, would stop walking about as if he owns the place. I admit he is a very handsome dog, but there are times when he takes his position here far too seriously, roaming about as if he was the head waiter. I just ignore him – after all, I am the customer.

Well, I can jump the stone stile easily, but some dogs might find it difficult, as it's quite high. My trick is to kick off from the little stone step on the left hand side, which reduces the height of the jump somewhat.

Helen does get rather edgy if there are cows in the first field, but I take no notice of them. They are harmless, besides I am much more interested in getting my paws into the river. This is not as easy as it sounds as a wire fence has been erected in front of the riverbank, probably to stop the cows from drowning. There are places where I can get into the river though, so I just have to be patient and wait until I reach them.

The kingfisher moments that Auntie Liz and Helen get so excited about are certainly spectacular. Even a border collie can appreciate that splendid flash of blue as it darts towards the water. I've yet to see the kingfisher emerge with a fish in its beak, but I have seen films on television that show it. There are loads of wild geese and ducks along this river bank too, but they usually nest on the other side and are not half as interesting or spectacular as the kingfisher.

over, you find yourself in the first of a series of fields that open out into each other. By keeping the river on your right you will eventually come to another stone stile that takes you onto the road that leads to Asthall. You can walk on, following the river for another half a mile or so, but we tend to turn at this point.

On returning to Swinbrook, it is well worth visiting St Mary's church near Swinford's village green. It's a superb 12th-century church in which you will discover ornate marble effigies in two triple tiers depicting six of the Fettiplace family who lived in this area for four centuries.

The Fleece,
Church Green, Witney

Because the River Windrush meanders gently through Witney, and the town's ancient church with its magnificent spire stands as a proud landmark for miles around, there's much to see and enjoy in this bustling market town which has adapted amazingly well to the 21st century. Whilst it has a 17th-century Butter Cross with a gabled roof, clock-turret and sundial, which stands in the middle of the Market Square, it has modern shopping areas too.

The Fleece is a fine Georgian building overlooking Witney's spacious Church Green at the southern end of the town. It was once the home of Clinch's brewery and now it's a lively gastropub which opens for breakfast at 8 a.m. and serves hot food all day.

Poetry lovers will no doubt be intrigued to know that the Fleece was

---

Pythius says

I really love this pub. The moment I arrive, a member of staff places a large bowl of cold water under the table and pats me on the head. Canines are allowed into the bar area where we can sit in front of the fire or by the window and enjoy a view of Church Green. At the rear (where I am not allowed to venture) I'm told there's a buzzing little restaurant decorated with Victorian-style mirrors and dark wood.

Because the Windrush, which flows right round the meadow, is quite shallow in parts, I am able jump in and out of the river, up and down the river banks and then dry off by rushing round the meadow. We do have to look out for livestock (which I don't like very much) as there are cows grazing here sometimes. But otherwise it's a doggie paradise.

Sometimes, if the weather is good, Helen takes me through a sort of tunnel, which is really a bridge for the A40. This leads to a man-made lake which was created when they built the A40 many years ago. This is doggie heaven too as there are lots of shallow bits where I can swim or simply splash in the water. We often circumnavigate this lake, ending up back at the tunnel. I reckon that if you allow for my little swims and sniffs along the way, it adds an extra hour to the walk.

a great favourite of Dylan Thomas during the year he lived in nearby South Leigh. It's said that he would cycle across country to Witney, stopping for a pint (or five) at the Fleece before heading home. That was in the late 1940s, when the Fleece was just a local pub. Now it serves excellent food, created from local produce where possible, and sustainable fish which is transported to Oxfordshire the moment it's landed by Scottish Skippers. This means customers are constantly surprised by the wide range of freshly-caught fish available as specials of the day. This is a pub where the menu follows the seasons faithfully, and where chefs slave over a hot stove rather than a microwave cooker. The coffee is good too.

The walk

Leave the Fleece, turn left and look for a turning on the left that takes you past the vets on the left-hand side and Sainsbury's car park on the right. At the main road and traffic lights, stop and wait, traffic is heavy and often travels too fast. Once you have crossed safely you will see a small pathway which leads to Witney's Lake and Meadow Country Park, which provides walkers with 75 acres of meadow in which to ramble. A large map detailing the paths and listing the wildlife you may see stands by the main gate.

The Woodstock Arms, Woodstock

The Woodstock Arms stands in Market Street, Woodstock. Although you can occasionally find a space to park close to the pub, it's probably easier to aim for the free public car park in nearby Hensington Road. Woodstock gets very busy at times, particularly during the tourist season.

The Woodstock Arms is a delight. The moment you open the main door and walk into its friendly atmospheric bar you know you are in for a treat. This pub occupies an area which was once three separate sites

---

Pythius says

Another town pub, but it's such a friendly place I can cope with that. In the summer we sit outside in the attractive little courtyard, but in the winter I aim for a table near the fire. The staff are always very friendly, and usually give me a pat when they come to take Helen's order, which is inevitably fish and chips. Apparently the pub serves the best fish and chips in Oxfordshire, though sadly I never get a chance to taste it, despite putting on my most appealing look.

Because I adore seeking out plastic bottles and encouraging Auntie Liz and Helen to throw them for me to catch, I enjoy this walk. No other walk we share offers so many bottles. They are in the bushes, on the side of the lane and simply everywhere. Empty cigarette and crisp packets litter the path too, but I ignore them. It's the bottles I like; they make a nice crackling noise when I bite into them. As you can imagine, Auntie Liz and Helen get really mad when I keep rushing into the bushes to find them. There is a little river that runs beside the lane for a while, but everything is so overgrown, even I don't enjoy splashing in the water as much as I normally do.

I guess I would give this walk five out of ten. It could be really beautiful, but no one seems to be caring for it as they should. Once I nearly cut my paw on a pile of glass that had been thrown into the grass beside the lane. Now why would someone walk all the way up this lane to throw glass panes away, when they could have been recycled? There are times when I don't understand humans at all.

dating back to the 16th century. Originally known as the Three Tuns it went on to be called the Duke of Wellington and then the Royal Oak. Over the centuries the building has undergone several internal changes.

Today's visitor will discover it's a warm and friendly building, illuminated with many candles and fresh flowers. Roaring log fires add their own touch of warmth during the winter. A picturesque courtyard at the rear, which is filled with greenery, offers visitors a respite from the crowds who throng Woodstock's streets during the summer.

Pythius is always welcome here and a bowl of chilled water is offered immediately, should he need it.

We come here for the food, freshly prepared on the premises from local produce and high quality fresh fish delivered daily from Brixham. If you want a pub meal to remember, try their fried cod, which is first soaked in beer and then coated with breadcrumbs and fried. We consider this dish one of the best cod and chips in the area. The real ales on tap are great too.

The walk

The walk begins in Union Street, beside the public car park. Walk down Union Street, turning right when you reach Brook Hill and head towards the cemetery in Green Lane (into which Brook Hill leads). Then it's a matter of going straight, straight, straight until a mile or so beyond the cemetery you reach the Roman road, Akeman Street, which will take you for as many miles as you wish to walk in either direction. This stretch of it is also on the Oxfordshire Way.

A tangled untamed wood abuts the lane for about a quarter of a mile. Unfortunately, the wood is not well cared for and a mass of litter can be found everywhere on the early part of the walk. Eventually the wood ends and you come to a point where the walk opens up into fields. A large oblong stone seat (a monument to Norman Taylor who died in 2006) offers you a chance to rest and enjoy the view.

We usually walk for about half a mile along this route and then return the way we came, but you can certainly extend the walk if you wish.

Pythius-Peacocke's last word

Well that's it folks – 40 walks – 40 pubs. It's been a great experience.

I have been welcomed and patted on the head, offered water and even given a few pigs' ears and Bonios during my travels. I have also explored some wonderful lanes, fields, meadows and woods, and been allowed to splash about in some superb rivers. I have also managed to give myself a few mud baths along the way.

The pubs we visited were chosen with care and they are all special in their own way. I admit that from time to time I encountered a really cold floor, or an exceptionally fluffy carpet, but we border collies can live with that, because in the end it is all about having a day out with my mistress and her friends.

We couldn't have finished this venture had it not been for dear Auntie Liz who takes me out for regular walks often and is very, very special. I have known her from the very first moment that I came to live with Helen. It was Auntie Liz who brought a bottle of champagne to our cottage on my arrival so that she and Helen could toast my future happiness.

Uncle John has been a real sport too. I like the fact that he is a really careful driver and always puts a blanket at the back of the car for me so that I can curl up and sleep when we drive home. And Auntie Kate, she must certainly not be forgotten. Gosh can she stride out when she wants to, a quite remarkable walker and a very good friend. Her dog Polly is a great companion too – we get along very well.

I would also like to say a big thank you to artist Sue Mynall who has spent hours in my company getting to know me, and so turn those special moments I have talked about into pictures.

I do hope that you enjoy the pubs and walks as much as I did. Pubs that welcome dogs are very special places and if we don't use them, we are going to lose them, and then there will be no way doggies like me can place our paws under the table.

Contact information

This information is as accurate as we could make it at the time of publication. We give website addresses wherever we could find them. We welcome corrections and additions for future editions of the book.

Bibury – The Swan Inn, 01285 740695 www.cotswold-inns-hotels.co.uk/swan
Binsey – The Perch Inn, 01865 728891 www.the-perch.co.uk
Bledington – The Kings Head Inn, 01608 658365 www.thekingsheadinn.net
Bourton-on-the-Water – The Kingsbridge Inn, 01451 824119
Broadway – The Crown and Trumpet, 01386 853202
                                                www.cotswoldholidays.co.uk
Burford – The Lamb Inn, 01993 823155 www.cotswold-inns-hotels.co.uk
Chadlington – The Tite Inn, 01608 676475 www.titeinn.com
Charlbury – The Bell – 01608 810278 www.bellhotel-charlbury.com
Chipping Campden – The Eight Bells, 01386 840371   www.eightbellsinn.co.uk
Chipping Norton – The Chequers, 01608 644717 www.chequers-pub.com
Church Hanborough – The Hand and Shears, 01993 881392
Clanfield – The Clanfield Tavern, 01367 810223 www.clanfieldtavern.com
Coates – The Tunnel House Inn, 01285 770280 www.tunnelhouse.com
Coleshill – The Radnor Arms, 01793 861575 www.theradnorarms.co.uk
Coln St Aldwyns – The New Inn, 01285 750651 www.new-inn.co.uk
Compton Abdate – Puesdown Inn, 01451 860262
                                                www.puesdown.cotswoldinns.com
Crawley – The Lamb Inn – 01993 703753 www.thelambcrawley.com
Ducklington – The Strickland Arms, 01993 703413
Eastleach Turville – The Victoria Inn, 01367 850277
Eynsham – The Queen's Head, 01865 881229 www.thequeenshead.net
Eynsham – The Talbot, 01865 881348 www.talbot-oxford.co.uk
Filkins – The Five Alls, 01367 860306
Finstock – The Plough Inn, 01993 868333 www.theplough-inn.co.uk
Great Rissington – The Lamb Inn – 01451 820388 www.thelambinn.com
Great Tew – The Falkland Arms, 01608 683653 www.falklandarms.org.uk
Kelmscott – The Plough, 01367 253543 www.ploughkelmscott.co.uk
Kemble – The Thames Head, 01285 770259 www.thamesheadinn.co.uk
Lechlade – The Swan Inn, 01367 253571 www.swanlechlade.co.uk
Marston – The Victoria Arms, 01865 241382 www.victoriaarms-marston.co.uk
North Hinksey – The Fishes, 01865 249796 www.fishesoxford.co.uk
North Leigh – The Woodman Inn, 01993 881790

Northleach – The Wheatsheaf, 01451 860244 www.cotswoldswheatsheaf.com
Oddington – The Fox Inn, 01451 870555 www.foxinn.net
Oxford – The Turf Tavern, 01865 243235 www.theturftavern.co.uk
Ramsdon – The Royal Oak, 01993 868213
Shilton – The Rose and Crown, 01993 842280
Stow-on-the-Wold – The Queen's Head, 01451 830563
Swinbrook – The Swan, 01993 823339 www.theswanswinbrook.co.uk
Witney – The Fleece, 01993 892270 www.fleecewitney.co.uk
Woodstock – The Woodstock Arms, 01993 811251 www.woodstockarms.co.uk